TWAYNE'S WORLD LEADERS SERIES

EDITORS OF THIS VOLUME

Arthur W. Brown

Baruch College, The City University

of New York

and

Thomas S. Knight

Adelphi University

B. F. Skinner

TWLS 63

B. F. Skinner

B. F. SKINNER

By JOHN A. WEIGEL
Miami University

TWAYNE PUBLISHERS

A DIVISION OF G. K. HALL & CO., BOSTON

Copyright©1977 by G. K. Hall & Co.
All Rights Reserved
First Printing

Library of Congress Cataloging in Publication Data

Weigel, John A.
  B. F. Skinner

  (Twayne's world leaders series; TWLS 63)
  Bibliography: p. 114-21
  Includes index.
  1. Skinner, Burrhus Frederic, 1904- 2. psy-
cologists-Biography. 3. Behaviorism 1. Title
BS109.S55W44   150'.19'4340924 (B)   77-1673
ISBN 0-8057-7713-X

For Milton White

Contents

About the Author

John A. Weigel is Professor of English at Miami University, Oxford, Ohio. With advanced degrees in literature (Western Reserve University) and psychology (Columbia University), he has both alternated and crossed fields. As a Ford Foundation Fellow in 1952 and 1953 he pioneered research in verbal behavior and information theory as a much-needed antidote to the then fashionable psychoanalysis of literature and literary figures.

Author of two critical biographies, *Lawrence Durrell* and *Colin Wilson* (Twayne's English Authors Series), as well as of numerous professional articles and light verses, he is now researching a book-length study of John Barth and a very brief treatise tentatively called "Conversations with the Dead." Dr. Weigel first met the controversial psychologist in 1947 at Columbia University where as a student in Professor Skinner's summer course in Verbal Behavior he was quickly converted to behaviorism. For thirty years, his ruling passion has been to explain B. F. Skinner to those who misjudge him because they do not understand his work.

Preface

Perhaps no justification for including the American psychologist B. F. Skinner among the distinguished leaders honored in this series is necessary. Originally, however, the series was confined to "Great Thinkers," a category which could not have embraced him without irony, for Skinner's commitment has been anathema to mentalists from the beginning of his career, when he seemed to empty not only rats but also humans of cognitive processes. Although one is relieved that Ralph Waldo Emerson, a great thinker honored in the former series, may now welcome Skinner into the hall of fame as a brother leader, some ambiguity still persists.

In these troubled times not all leaders are beyond suspicion. Anxious searchers after quick solutions to pressing problems are often too desperate—quietly or otherwise—to check the credentials of prophets unworthy of their trust. It is the contention of this study that B. F. Skinner is a true prophet, one whose credentials are beyond reproach. All mootness in the Skinner projection has to do with the mootness of science itself and not with Skinner as a man or as a scientist. The questions are clear, if still unanswered. Shall there be, can there be, should there be a *science* of human behavior?

If human beings ultimately prove to be inscrutable, so that a science of human behavior is silly or irrelevant, no one other than scientists themselves are presently enfranchised to make that discovery. Thus it is both ethical and logical to let scientists go on systematically scrutinizing human behavior until either scrutability or inscrutability is certified as fact. Everyone wants and respects a fact when it is available without too much trouble. The murkiness begins either when facts are not easily comprehended by laymen or when they challenge venerable traditions.

This study tries to establish the facts. At the same time no attempt is made here to avoid partisanship. I have been convinced for a long time that Skinner is a good and true prophet and that as such he has been often maligned because he has been misunderstood. I have tried to communicate my convictions to the nonspecialist and thus have sometimes resorted, no doubt, to editorializing. If my enthusiasm has distorted Skinner's facts, I alone am guilty. Skinner may be a heretic, but he is not a petty liar. In any event, it is my contention here that B. F. Skinner has profoundly changed the world—and for the better—even if much of the world does not know it. He is, it seems to me, a rare kind of prophet, one who is in possession of both facts and vision.

I am grateful to the following students and friends—categories not necessarily mutually exclusive—for help with this book: Peter Buirski, John Watson, Celia Shapiro Bergsman, Jill Frederick, Beth Tobin and Kathy Keho Chafetz. Professor Skinner has graciously accepted my attempt to honor him without in any way being responsible for this text, which he has not seen. I have been working on this study for over a decade. Everytime I thought my manuscript was well-rounded off, Professor Skinner produced another major work. Now that he has begun to publish his memoirs, I feel I need wait no longer. I have, however, tried not to compete with my prophet. My book is definitely a "secondary work." Skinner's words are still prime, and thus anyone interested in my study will greatly benefit further from consulting Professor Skinner's quite readable books.

JOHN A. WEIGEL

Miami University
Oxford, Ohio

Acknowledgments

Permission to quote from *About Behaviorism, Beyond Freedom and Dignity,* and *Particulars of My Life* has been granted by the publisher, Alfred A. Knopf, Inc. Permission to quote from *Science and Human Behavior* and *Walden Two* has been granted by the publisher, Macmillan Publishing Company, Inc.

Chronology

1904   Burrhus Frederick Skinner is born March 20, in Susquehanna, Pennsylvania, to respectable, middle-class, Protestant parents.

1910   Family's purchase of a Ford climaxes early childhood.

1922   Graduated second in class of seven from same high school parents had attended, followed by matriculation at Hamilton College.

1923   Sudden death of younger and only brother tests Skinner's objectivity.

1926   Receives A.B. degree from Hamilton College with Phi Beta Kappa and reputation as campus literateur and rebel.

1927   Abandons career as a writer for sojourn in Greenwich Village, trip abroad, and admission to Harvard Graduate School to study psychology.

1931   Ph.D. from Harvard is followed by three years as National Research Council Fellow and two years as Harvard Junior Fellow.

1936   Accepts first teaching job, University of Minnesota, and marries Yvonne Blue.

1938   First major publication, *The Behavior of Organisms: An Experimental Analysis*, is based on Harvard doctoral dissertation.

1945   Becomes member of faculty and sometime Chairman of Department of Psychology, Indiana University.

1948   Returns to Harvard as Professor of Psychology and publishes *Walden Two*.

1953   Publication of *Science and Human Behavior*, designed as text to supplement *Walden Two* and *The Behavior of Organisms*, advances career.

1957   Productive time: publishes *Verbal Behavior* and *Schedules of Reinforcement* (with Charles B. Ferster).

1958   Receives honors: appointment at Harvard as Edgar Pierce Professor, recipient of Distinguished Scientific Award from American Psychological Association.

1961　Publishes *The Analysis of Behavior* (with James G. Holland) and *Cumulative Record*.

1968　Publishes *The Technology of Teaching*, a collection of earlier articles with several new additions.

1969　Publication of *Contingencies of Reinforcement: A Theoretical Analysis*, marks the beginning of a more philosophical orientation.

1971　Publication of controversial *Beyond Freedom and Dignity* is followed by storm of protests.

1974　Publishes *About Behaviorism*, an attempt to answer critics.

1976　*Particulars of My Life*, first volume of autobiography, is praised for its nostalgia.

CHAPTER 1

The Cumulative Record

THE name of Burrhus Frederick Skinner is usually abbreviated to B. F. Skinner by professional colleagues, to Fred Skinner by personal friends, and to *that Skinner* by hostile critics. Dedicated followers are known as Skinnerians. They are the proud victims of a legion of enemies who would burn them as witches or otherwise annihilate them for their sins of rejecting both God and humanity. Humanists have declared an endless open season on Skinnerians, who allegedly hide in Skinner boxes in which they train themselves, their children, and innocent students as if they were all animals in an experiment. Skinnerians are often denounced as behaviorists, who in turn are often accused of being Skinnerians. Genus and species are confounded in the sport of beating the academic bushes to find these creatures, who, nevertheless, have persistently survived and even multiplied exceedingly although often in a considerably mutated form.

I *The Skinner Box*

It is an undeniable fact that B. F. Skinner is guilty of having invented the box which bears his name. He is also guilty of defining "behavior" in such a way that it can be observed, described, and—as a result—also predicted. "By behavior, then," Skinner wrote in 1938, "I mean simply the movement of an organism or of its parts in a frame of reference provided by the organism itself or by various external objects or fields of force."[1] Quite undramatically, the infamous Skinner box is an ingenious device for focusing the "behavior" of both subject (animal or human) and experimenter (always human) on the subject's pressing of a lever or otherwise manipulating the environment to achieve identifiable effects. The lever pressing or other manipulations may or may not, depending

15

on the schedule designed by the experimenter, release into an accessible place in the box a modest-sized pellet of food or some other desirable object. Many little events in the boxed-in environment of the subject, which is usually a rat in the classical experiments, "reinforce" the lever-pressing behavior—that is, make it likely to happen again. The main controlling event, however, is the patterning of the arrival in the subject's environment of something which impresses the subject favorably and which the subject has earned in some way that he can occasionally repeat in order to be rewarded again. It is really as simple as that: rats and people work for what satisfies them.

Skinner's early experiments concentrated on the behavior of one rat. When the rat in the box, for example, had been deprived of food Skinner noted that it was inclined to eat each pellet of food that appeared in an accessible tray as the result of the rat's pressing a lever—that is, as the result of something the rat had done to its environment. The animal was presumably pleased enough thereafter to press the lever again, sometimes without getting any food immediately, depending upon the experimenter's plans and the rat's patience—the latter being the rat's need for the food rather than some abstraction such as courage or discipline. Skinner avoided value judgments on the rat's behavior and refrained from praising or blaming the rat for what it was doing. Because he was in control of the delivery of food, which to the rat is an effective kind of reward, Skinner was accused of manipulating the behavior of his subject rather than teaching it. The charge is true enough, and the fact that Skinner did not try to lecture to his rats but rather fed them according to various schedules is quite significant. Later he was to advocate a similar technology of education for humans.

The *strength* of the animal's lever pressing or any other designated habit is measured as resistance to extinction of that habit. In general, the more erratic the arrival of the reward the longer the subject will persist in pressing the lever or doing whatever it must do in order to receive satisfaction. A rat has been trained to sit before a lever and press it again and again, sometimes very rapidly, with no apparent "hope" of receiving even one pellet of food until the animal has performed hundreds of pressings. Such persistence resembles faith: the animal has been persuaded to work hard for only a few randomly distributed answers to its prayerlike pressings! The fact that such behavior in rats resembles religious behavior in humans annoys philanthropists more than it does rodent-lovers, for faith has been considered an exclusively human attribute. So far rats have not objected to the analogy but have gone on working very hard for few rewards—just as humans do.

Sensible rats, of course, would stop pressing the lever soon after no food appeared. Presumably, sensible men would do the same. It is a fact that most men stop putting coins into a vending machine that ejects no merchandise. The machine is broken, such men say. They lose their faith in it quickly. Insouciantly they seek out other machines. Fortunately, neither rats nor men are always so simply sensible. Poets, for example, "emit verbal responses" that produce few tangible pellets of food or few food surrogates such as dollars.

Lever pressing and poetry writing differ significantly in that the former is less complex and thus more easily measured. Acknowledging such significant differences, good psychologists never confound humans and animals; neither do they reverse the direction of their concerns and study men in order to understand rats. Ultimately always altruistic, they study rats in order to begin to understand men. Most scientists have kept their own heads while occasionally decorticating rodents and canines. As a result, behavioral psychology has become more sophisticated. Pavlov's discovery that dogs could be conditioned to drool at the sound of a bell by associating the sound with the sight and smell of food was only the beginning. However, such a simple substitution, bell for meat, is often the layman's only idea of "conditioning." Anyone knows that, although dogs do not eat bells, they do hear bells; therefore, since hearing bells is an acceptable bit of behavior in a real universe, no one objects to making dogs drool at bells ringing. It is only a trick.

II   *Operant Conditioning*

Skinner's pioneer experiments emphasized what he named operant conditioning to distinguish it from Pavlovian or instrumental conditioning, which is virtually only the establishing of a simple reflex. Importantly, operant conditioning leads to the kind of behavior which persists because it is effective and not merely because it has been somehow stamped in. The identification and manipulation of the variables involved in this kind of conditioning made a rigorous science of *human* behavior possible for the first time. *The Behavior of Organisms* (1938) is the complete record of the young Skinner's systematic observation of certain controllable aspects of the behavior of *one* rat confined to *one* box. The rebellious graduate student boldly broke with traditional animal psychology in choosing to study the behavior of one rat rather than a group of rats. Before Skinner's experiment it had been customary to get smooth curves by averaging the performances of many subjects. Skinner, however, set out to "train" just one organism, carefully defining before he began those aspects of his subject's behavior he was going to observe. He knew that in general the behavior he was interested in was related to the environment; but because the whole "outside world" lay beyond the scope of his powers of observation, he frankly limited the environment of his subject by putting it into a small but not uncomfortable box. That limitation was a happy idea, for it facilitated the experimenter's observing and recording important data. The lever pressings of the rat, for example, could be recorded on a revolving drum by a stylus connected to the lever. The drum revolved at a steady rate so that the marks made by the stylus would be closer together the faster the pressing, farther apart the slower the pressing. It was easy to arrange the mechanism so that the stylus jumped up a constant space for every pressing and recorded only a horizontal line between pressings. Each lever pressing was thus recorded on the chart as a step-up in a line. The time of no-pressings was recorded as a straight line. Obviously the slope of each line recording could be used as a measure of the rate of responding. It was all very neat, and novel only in its application to the behavior of a living organism.

Skinner insisted as early as 1938 on the validity of his method for studying human behavior as well as animal behavior. In all fairness he also tried to view his own behavior with the same objectivity. He knew that his kind of psychology would be controversial. He knew that he was not only breaking with Freudian and Gestalt traditions but also significantly modifying the Watsonian and Pavlovian heresies. He did not set out to irritate or shock his professors and predecessors. He simply behaved as he had to under the circumstances.

III   *Of Rats and Men*

Long before Skinner, early psychologists had tried to find a rationale and a methodology for "thinkers" eager to check on their intuitions, but not until the emergence of a new discipline ponderously called "experimental physiological psychology" did they openly underwrite objective experimentation instead of introspection. Even traditional philosophers and cozy humanists could honor the qualifier "experimental" as a guarantee of truthfulness in certain physiological research, but they still believed—or hoped—that the human "psyche" was beyond the reach of experimentation. A human being surely could not be, or at least should not be, studied as if he were an animal. For many, the unpleasant connotations of atheism and blasphemy still cling to all psychologies. It is not only theologians who insist on a transcendental factor in all equations describing human behavior. Both unsophisticated and literate humans overwhelmingly oppose "tampering" with people and operations.

Even historians do not easily distinguish between various kinds of psychology, much less know how to evaluate them. Certainly, popular opinions of what it is all about have become more and more confused. Currently, however, several correlated clusters of psychological thinking and procedures are sufficiently dissimilar from one another to be described as "schools." Depth psychologies, for example, all share being looked upon with suspicion by nondepth psychologists. Capitalized nouns vie with lowercase descriptive words for preeminence, but Gestalt and Psychoanalysis are usually grouped together as "deep," a category from which all behavioral sciences as well as behaviorism (or Behaviorism, if one is formal) are proudly excluded despite periodic attempts by neobehaviorists to analyze behavior in depth and occasional forays by humanistic philosophers into the laboratory. That "lab" was once dominated by an orthodox trinity, namely, Structuralism (Wundt, et al.), Functionalism (Dewey, Woodworth, et al.), and Associationism (Pavlov, Thorndike, et al.). Wundt and Pavlov experimented with dogs, Thorndike with cats. They were all more or less interested in people, too, but cautious in their extrapolations from animals to humans. More recently a new kind of trinity has emerged, in which the dominant group claims to have resolved the distinction between deep and behavioral methodologies. A third force has been postulated, one which is as real as intuition and introspection on one level and as real as overt behavior on another level—the kind of awareness which accepts introspections and external events as only two of the determinants of real reality—the world of *all* awareness, a third world. This new trinity is literally a three-in-one concept. As bad at adding as theologians, the third-world philosopher-psychologists agree in rejecting behavioral psychology as a naive "rat psychology."

Although a clever cartoon once fantasied a laboratory rat exulting at its success in conditioning a human experimenter, in real life rats have not yet verbalized their reactions to being manipulated. Most humans, on the other hand, have been clamorously indignant at being treated as if they were rats. They have been conditioned to fear conditioning. Among the villains that they are sure want to condition them, they are likely to name Skinner first. Although Skinner's concerns long ago escalated from rats to humans, he is still the most infamous of the *rat* psychologists. When a scientist is called a *rat* psychologist the implication is that he has reduced humans to rats—or more rarely, that he has tried to elevate rats to humans. To the many who reject behavioral science Skinner inevitably became the prime Public Enemy. Called both Fascist and Communist, he has been attacked by representatives of institutions from under which he has tried to pull rug or Rock. Unaware that they are demonstrating the validity of Skinner's concepts, anxious opponents of a science of human behavior refuse to consider seriously that brave new world first discovered in the Skinner box. Their passionate opposition is often inversely proportional to their knowledge of Skinner's work. "Man," they say emphatically, "is not a rat!"

In any event there is only one universe, Skinner or no Skinner. The small experimental universe in which rats, pigeons, and humans are variously subjected to operant conditioning in order that the experimenter may refine his knowledge about how certain organisms behave and how that behavior can be altered, is only part of a bigger universe in which larger and certainly often more important events take place, such as the birth, life, and death of human beings. Yet the smaller parts of the universe take up most of man's time and concern, and in that small space everyone has always more or less tried to manipulate other organisms that impinge upon him. Humans train their pet animals to obey. They control their pets' environment in such a way as to keep the house tidy and the animals more or less content. No one minds the fact that dogs are conditioned to shake hands—a silly thing for a dog to learn, really—and most people would prefer that their children use the bathroom rather than the neighbor's yard at toilet time. Children are taught how to behave, animals are trained. Allegedly, children are educated in principles which they are free to apply or not to apply. They must pay penalties if they do not respect freedom of choice; that is, they are held responsible for what they do no matter how they have been in fact trained. Also, presumably humans can observe their pets' habits objectively and predict with some accuracy just what the pets are going to do next. Allegedly, however, it is bad taste if not inhuman to predict what one's friends are going to do next as the result of past observations of their habits.

IV *John Watson*

Without John Watson's work and ideas Skinner might have been delayed. It was Watson who first radicalized psychology. He asked an awesomely simple question: "Why don't we make what we can *observe* the real field of psychology? Let us limit ourselves to things that can be observed, and formulate laws concerning only those things. Now what can we observe? We can observe *behavior—what the organism does or says.* And let us point out at once: that *saying* is doing—that is, *behaving.* Speaking overtly or to ourselves (thinking) is just as objective a type of behavior as baseball."[2]

Furthermore, John Watson did not abdicate the responsibility to do something about the universe he was observing. "The interest of the behaviorist in man's doings," he wrote, "is more than the interest of the spectator—he wants to control man's reactions as physical scientists want to control and manipulate other natural phenomena. It is the business of behavioristic psychology to be able to predict and to control human activity. To do this it must gather scientific data by experimental methods. Only then can the trained behaviorist predict, given the stimulus, what reaction will take place; or, given the reaction, state what the situation or stimulus is that has caused the reaction."[3]

Skinner has, of course, considerably refined Watson's position. The contemporary behaviorist admits the reality, for example, of consciousness not as a capitulation to introspectionists but as an extension of the areas properly to be observed scientifically. Skinner first spelled out these refinements in an important essay in 1963, "Behaviorism at Fifty," and reconciled without embarrassment the extended interests of the new behaviorism with the old, noting "that a science of behavior [must] face the problem of privacy," while insisting, however, that science "can deal with these [private] events without assuming that they have any special nature or must be known in any special way. The skin is not that important as a boundary. Private and public events have the same kinds of physical dimensions."[4]

Most behavioral scientists no longer reject the reality of inner events, but they are wary of imputing causes to nonobservables. A concept need not be rejected simply because that concept has been traditionally called "subjective" or "mental." Although the passage between the Scylla of mentalism and the Charybdis of ratism has been opened, let the pilot beware. Despite the permissiveness of latter-day behaviorists, Skinner has remained a rigorous scientist. As he widened and deepened the scope of his concerns, he has become more philosophical and has speculated about social problems. Yet he has insisted that psychology must be rigorously objective no matter what new and rebellious forces may try to add in the way of humanistic concerns.

V   *Biographer of a Behaviorist*

A man's life is not a fiction. Whatever else it may be it is always true. A biography, however, is a construct, and as such it is necessarily never the *whole* Truth. An honest biographer hopes that his account of his subject's life is sufficient unto the need. He knows it is never necessary, for people are born and die quite efficiently without being the subject of biographies. Furthermore, there is a special problem in summarizing the facts of Skinner's life. Traditional biographers try to explain *how* and *why* the subject was what he was and did what he did. They generally divide the *how* between impersonal (genetic) and personal (environmental) determinants, and the *why* between character traits the subject was responsible for and acts of God that no one could help but which often are quite efficient in altering behavior. Thus the conventional biographer usually praises his subject for his valiant resistance to determinants before which lesser men would have faltered, commending him and giving him his due credit for how and why he used his inheritance *against* his environment to good advantage. Since Skinner has consistently viewed his own life as objectively as he has observed his rats, and since he gives credit for his achievements to neither freedom nor dignity—in the pre-Skinner sense of those terms—he should be treated here simply as a behaving organism doing precisely what was completely predictable under the circumstances if all the circumstances were known. Logically, there is no *why* about a behaviorist. There is only a behaving man, and so the biographer need only identify the contingencies—the *how*. Some compromise (following Skinner's own compromise) is obviously needed, for the subject of this life-sketch cannot be confined to a laboratory.

The sequence of events known as "Skinner's life" is the cumulative record of achievements which were reinforcing to the subject and thus resistant to extinction. Plotting total number of words against the years 1930 - 1960, Skinner has himself demonstrated that his productivity for that thirty-year period was fairly constant. The "curve" shows a constant slope.[5] When requested by "Project A" of the American Psychological Association in the late 1950s to cooperate with other "proprietors" of "current systems of psychology" who had agreed to "describe their wares," Skinner honestly could not respond in the same idiom. Instead he submitted a paper he had written earlier, "A Case History in Scientific Method." In the preparatory note to the reprint of this paper in the 1961 edition of *Cumulative Record*, Skinner defended his position while admitting its difficulties. "A scientist is an extremely complex organism, and his behavior is likely to resist to the very last any effort toward an empirical analysis. Nevertheless, if anything useful is to be said about him, either in trying to understand his behavior or in inculcating similar behavior in others, it will be in the nature of an empirical rather than a formal analysis."[6]

VI *Early Years*

Burrhus Frederick Skinner was born March 20, 1904, in Susquehanna, Pennsylvania. In the first volume of his recent autobiography, *Particulars of My Life* (1976), and in an earlier, informal sketch the mature Skinner retrospectively identifies those influences which helped shape his life, not neglecting to credit contingencies and luck with those reinforcing qualities one would expect a behaviorist to recognize. Although he avoids a tedious translation of the literary vernacular into behavioral jargon, he honors a behaviorist's obligation to be as objective as possible about his own acts, decisions, and crises—those events which plot lifelines. Evaluating his experiences as effective and thus reinforcing or as ineffective and thus eventually negligible, without conceit and without deception, he projects an image of himself as a successful person. Not surprisingly, Skinner emerges as an understandable man without regard to the observer's ultimate judgment of his value and his place in history.

Although more of an environmentalist than a geneticist, Skinner describes conscientiously certain characteristics of his immediate forebears that he probably inherited. His mother, Grace Burrhus (her maiden name became his first name) "was rated something of a beauty."[7] She was musical and although not quite top professional she was comfortably adequate as an accompanist and as a contralto singer. She was personally popular and certainly not illiterate. Skinner's father, a lawyer, was only moderately and erratically prosperous. The household was essentially middle-class Protestant, underwritten by the usual ethics and a straining for continuity with the past as well as an awareness of the communality available in a small Pennsylvania city. It was a simple matter of fact that Skinner should graduate from the same high school his parents had attended.

Grandmother Burrhus had an ancestor who served under Washington, and her husband had fought in the Civil War. According to Skinner she "read a great deal of fiction" and often reinforced her grandson's behavior with pie, candy, and letting him win at dominoes (16). His paternal grandparents, equally important genetically—by definition at least—also reinforced certain habits in the lad. Grandmother Skinner, who had always aspired to being a lady, intended that her son should become significant. Skinner notes, however, that "the aspirations she gave her son cost him dearly" (8). She also tried to indoctrinate her grandson in the terrors of hell. On the other hand, Grandfather Skinner "had absolutely no ambition. . . . He read the newspapers closely and loved politics and baseball" (10).

All in all Skinner's childhood was relatively secure. Homey details which he remembers nostalgically include the birth of a brother in 1906, the gift of his first Teddy Bear, and the family's purchase of a Ford in 1910. Checkers, dominoes, and a spelling board were favorite games in the Skinner, pre-TV household. Although he and his younger brother suspended belief in Santa Claus precociously early, they still enjoyed the usual holidays. The man to whom the boy was father writes in 1976 that he remembers "lying awake on New Year's eve, 1910, regretting the passing of that year with its lovely round number" (32). The observation escapes sentimentality by a safe margin, for 1910 was really the last of the nicely rounded years, to be followed by abrasive years of wars, depressions, and social upheavals, all of which endorsed a new moral permissiveness. Skinner's father went so far as to purchase Havelock Ellis' *Studies in the Psychology of Sex,* but not so far as not to keep it locked up in his office out of the sight of his young sons at home.

For the time being, however, young Skinner's environment remained stable. Indeed, it was, as he recalls, "a bountiful world, in which many wonderful things were to be had for the asking" (51). The boy's seedtime was fair: "Susquehanna was a dirty, unkempt town, but the great sweep of the river valley was magnificent. There were fields and pastures on the inner bank. . . . In spring we knew where to find the delicate trillium, arbutus, fringed gentian, and jack-in-the-pulpit . . ." (51). The youth's heart leaped up, it seems, in true Wordsworthian responses to Nature. "It was a world," Skinner reminisces, "we shared with animals." He owned a "cage-like mousetrap that caught mice alive" which he also used to trap chipmunks. He admits that he was unable to "tame" the chipmunks and some other animals. "Not much could be done with frogs, toads, or lizards, but turtles were easy to catch . . ." (52). There is a gentle irony in the normal pastimes of the boy who was eventually to be denounced as Satanic in his equating of animals and humans. The lad seems only moderately precocious and more than moderately innocent. Skinner remembers that he and his friends "enjoyed a peaceful coexistence" (83). Apparently he never attacked a schoolmate physically nor was he attacked by others. His gentleness, however, was tempered by his predilection for playing practical jokes. On Halloween, for example, he and his companions offered their victims no choice between trick or treat. They always tricked. Skinner admits that "there was no way to buy us off" (83).

Adolescence included scouting, summer camps, and some desultory piano lessons from a local teacher (who sucked Sen Sens and used doubtful reinforcement techniques such as jabbing the lad in the ribs with a pencil whenever he made a mistake). Young Skinner also showed considerable interest in art, drafting, and writing poetry and stories. He credits Miss Graves, his English teacher, for his becoming involved with literature. She was not any more successful, however, in making him accept her liberal deity than Grandmother Skinner had been in promoting her stern God. Just once he thought he had received a "divine message," but the experience was never repeated and his belief in God was extinguished early in his life, never to reappear even in those courteous concessions intellectuals often make.

Skinner's cheerful acceptance of an existence without supernatural events cleared his vision for things to be observed that were

there to be observed. His curiosity about life and its many observable complexities kept him alive and healthy. He found out early
that he was clever at inventing things, that he could plan and im-
plement his plans. He always enjoyed building his own apparatus,
for example, and although he is seldom perceived as creative, he
never doubted his own ability to project his interest from the
already known to those unknowns that might some day be known.
This ability, of course, is precisely what poets and mystics praise as
"imagination." The fact that the young Skinner worked intensely
and protractedly on the design of a perpetual motion machine
without ever getting it to work, indicates that he was capable of
striving for impossible goals, behavior similar to that of all questers
after dreams. Nevertheless, one must assume that Skinner *believed*
for a while that he *could* invent such a machine, for otherwise he
would have given up. In Skinnerian jargon, his habit of working on
a perpetual motion machine took some time to extinguish;
therefore, there must have been some earlier and effective reinforcement. Behaviorists do not believe in heroism as such. Persistence in the face of bad odds is always a function of contingencies
rather than the result of asserting one's will. It is well to remember
that if one says that Skinner "persevered" or "made a wise choice,"
one is translating from one jargon into another. Actually, the
mature Skinner was as inevitable as any impersonal event; thus his
decisions are often coolly delineated by those who respect his position *vis a vis* reality. Skinner's career unfolds as lawfully as the
eating habits of his rats, once the parameters are identified.

Skinner says he always liked school. What he means, of course, is
that he acted effectively in an academic environment and also felt
good there. He did not necessarily first feel good and then act effectively, nor *vice versa*. The two, good feeling and effectiveness,
simply correlate. (Indeed, they may be synonymous rather than
functions of one another.) As a student he frequently spent extra
time in the library and laboratories. Although there was no
bookstore in town, he did considerable reading on his own. While
still in high school he decided that Bacon had written the plays attributed to Shakespeare—not an original idea but certainly an unusual decision for an American teenager to make. He also read and
listened to the banalities in the local paper and on the radio, still not
quite sure how right or how wrong such ethical preachments might
turn out to be. He remembers that he was impressed by a
philosopher-columnist who advised his readers to clean up their

thoughts, to work hard, and reminded them: "Tomorrow is your friend" (161).

The Protestant ethic at home reinforced the schoolboy for working at odd jobs in his free hours. His most serious job was in the Economy Shoe Store, where he virtually became the manager for a time, so efficiently did he handle responsibility. The same ethic complicated his early relationship with girls, relationships which Skinner himself honestly and respectfully describes in some detail in his autobiography. Sufficient unto the purpose of this summary is the observation that Skinner without much delay first emerged adequately as lover, then eventually as husband and father. His early exploration of human sex behavior was not as objective as his observation of animal behavior; nevertheless—or perhaps therefore—he seems to have enjoyed his own sexuality more than most adult contemporaries whose trauma are boasted of in their writings and have colored their professional activities. In any event, Skinner's "life" survived, as it were, the usual crises.

VII   *Hamilton College*

After graduating second in a class of seven from high school, Skinner proceeded on schedule to college as most young men of his socioeconomic group did, and that same year his family moved to Scranton to an improved financial and social status. Skinner's collegiate "choice" was Hamilton College in Clinton, New York, a relatively small men's school with a good reputation and some significant social distinctions on campus. Skinner says the first mistake he made was to join a local rather than a national fraternity, and thus he had to live "at the foot of College Hill" (193). He had great hopes, however, for what college would mean to him. He really believed that youths wanted and obtained an education at such places.

The curriculum at Hamilton College stressed foreign languages, so Skinner studied Greek, Latin, French, and Spanish while majoring in English. He began to be described as "an aspiring young poet" (203) and also was considered conceited because of his insensitivity to the prevailing campus culture that did not believe in studying. He began to discover loneliness and its uses. While still in grade school he had written poems and stories, which he sometimes printed himself. He had even started a novel and had worked on the school paper. At college he began to contribute poems to the campus literary magazine. "I remember," he says gently in his autobiography, "walking the streets in physical pain for the lack of someone to put my arms around. Poetry may have helped" (207).

By the spring of his freshman year he had taken at least two giant steps toward a less idealistic future. The sudden death of his younger and only brother upset his parents deeply and permanently, although Skinner testifies that he "submitted to the tragic loss with little or no struggle" (209). He was beginning to perceive facts objectively, itself a fact about his perception that predicted his becoming a scientist. The apparent coolness of his stance in the face of the family tragedy was a measure of his growing awareness that neither accidents nor plans-gone-astray are necessarily deep mysteries to be correlated with an ineffable Providence.

Further evidence of his maturing skepticism toward romanticism and mysticism appeared in a final composition he wrote for his freshman course in college. The assignment was to assess the first year of college. (The instructor kept the themes and returned them to his students when they were seniors.) Skinner's opinion of college had been considerably altered as the result of just one academic year. His innocence and faith had yielded to experimental evidence almost at once: "It needed barely one month of the first term to show the boy he had misjudged college. There was no majority of students who enjoyed study, who frequented the library voluntarily" (211).

Not surprisingly, the young student returned to the campus the fall of his sophomore year prepared to make some adjustments to reality. His "main advance" that year was "extra-curricular" (216). He became friends with certain faculty members to whom he pays gracious tribute, among them in particular Dean Percy Saunders and his family. Visits with these informed people set the occasion quite literally for alterations in the young man's behavior. At the Saunders' house he met writers, musicians, and artists—a brave new world full of beautiful and bright people not many of whom were intimidated by either a Protestant ethic or a vengeful deity.

Although diffident toward academic pomposities and always willing to parody campus traditions, Skinner easily made Phi Beta Kappa in his junior year. During the summer recess before his senior year he enrolled in a writers' conference at Breadloaf, Vermont, where young and mature writers come together annually to reinforce one another. For many years Robert Frost had reigned there as the famous and infallible prophet-poet. When Skinner was asked by Frost to extend their summer contact and keep sending him samples of his writing, Skinner forwarded three short stories. After a suitable delay, a delay which made the reinforcement even more effective, Frost encouraged the aspirant to become a professional writer. The positive reinforcement from Frost was decisive, and near the end of his senior year the young man announced his decision to his family. In a solemn letter his father had earlier warned him against the writing profession but had also offered to help him with practical arrangements should he persist in testing his dream. Skinner agreed to test his talent for a year—to try to write in a study in the family attic. It did not take him a full year to realize that his writing did not meet his own expectations. He finally compromised by doing much significant reading and accepting a commission from his father to compose a digest of labor-management crises in the coal industry, an area which concerned his father as a lawyer representing management. The work, which Skinner conscientiously completed, was privately printed. Skinner's *first* publication was not *The Behavior of Organisms* (1938) after all, but instead a ponderous book grandly titled *A Digest of Decisions of the Anthracite Board of Conciliation*. Although his father was listed as coauthor, Skinner received the payment, which was enough money, Skinner notes, to open "fresh prospects for a career" (287). First, however, he granted himself a fling in New York City, where he quickly assimilated and enjoyed the bohemian habits of Greenwich Village.

After several months of "freedom" in the Village Skinner also enjoyed a time alone in Europe before returning (with less enjoyment) first class with his parents. In the fall he enrolled in the Harvard Graduate School to study psychology. Having decided that he failed as a writer because he had nothing important to say and also because literature was no longer viable, Skinner was not to return to creative fiction until he used the form in *Walden Two* to encase his vision of the Good Life attainable through science.

Skinner did not come to psychology as an instant convert. He had been reading extensively in so-called psychological literature. He had discovered John B. Watson and along with Bertrand Russell had dismissed Kant as "a mere misfortune" (298). Like Russell, he was impatient with anything not relatively factual. Rejecting philosophical speculations and metaphysical assumptions, the young Skinner opted for Watson and Russell perhaps too enthusiastically at first. "It would be a long time," he observed later, "before I saw the mistake which Russell and Watson were making" (299). That mistake had to do with conditioning and was eventually rectified by Skinner's discovery of *operant* conditioning as more or less the equivalent of free will and much more prevalent than Pavlovian conditioning.

In November of 1927 an article by H. G. Wells in the *New York Times* became definitive for the young man. In appraising George Bernard Shaw, Wells had downgraded the dramatist relative to Professor Pavlov, the Russian scientist. "Pavlov is a star which lights the world, shining above a vista hitherto unexplored," Wells had concluded. Skinner also abandoned Shaw, his old symbol of literature, for Pavlov, his new symbol of science: "And why should *I* hesitate?" he asked himself. "There was no reason at all. It was to be graduate study in psychology" (301).

VIII   *Graduate School and Early Career*

Skinner's self-imposed schedule as a graduate student seems fantastic to anyone not committed to sainthood or martyrdom—or both. For two years, he "would rise at six, study until breakfast, go to classes, laboratories, and libraries with no more than fifteen minutes unscheduled during the day, study until exactly nine o'clock at night and go to bed."[8] For recreation he played the piano—Bach fugues! He had few "dates" but instead filled in on subjects he needed. "To pass statistics," Skinner notes quietly, "I simply read G. Uldney Yule's *An Introduction to the Theory of Statistics.*"[9]

Skinner generously credits several of his teachers and several of his fellow students at Harvard with reinforcing the direction and the intensity of his work. He soon learned the implications of his new commitment to *scientific* psychology. Instead of keeping his focus on philosophy, as earlier students of psychology had been advised, he informed no less an authority than Professor Whitehead that a "psychological epistemology" was now needed.[10] Obviously the student was neither ingratiating nor cooperative. In fact, he produced such an unorthodox thesis for his doctorate that it was rejected by the chairman of his committee, Professor E. G. Boring. The young rebel had experimented with the behavior of only one rat, and specifically the changes in the rate of eating of that one rat under controlled and observable conditions. He had radically simplified procedures in order to obtain equally radically simplified data leading to the *discovery*—the word is not used casually here—of a new kind of conditioning. Characteristically, after being rejected, Skinner did not rework his "thesis." He simply resubmitted it without changes to a new committee to which Boring graciously had not nominated himself. The work, which eventually became *The Behavior of Organisms* (1938), was approved by the new committee but not as enthusiastically as years later when Skinner was invited to return to Harvard as a member of the faculty.

After receiving the Ph.D. from Harvard, Skinner survived for two years on fellowships from the National Research Council, during which time he studied and experimented on his own. Three more years as a Junior Fellow at Harvard completed his apprentice years, and in 1936 he accepted a full-time teaching position at the University of Minnesota. It was his first experience in front of a classroom, and he worked hard to keep ahead of his students. He did, however, persuade a significant number of his students originally committed to other disciplines to change to psychology. Among the converts of whom Skinner was proud were Norman Gutman and W. K. Estes.

Meanwhile the young scientist had not completely lost interest in literature. In 1934 he published an article in *The Atlantic Monthly* about Gertrude Stein, then a highly controversial writer. Skinner claimed that Miss Stein's "secret" was simply that she had experimented with automatic writing.[11] This sally into literary criticism was symptomatic of Skinner's more than casual concern with all kinds of human verbal behavior, and his assumption that even literary behavior could be productively studied and experimented with was to lead later to attacks on the mystique of creativity traditionally assumed to be beyond the sight and ken of mere scientists. If the young researcher was brash he was also a good scientist. By the end of 1935 the name B. F. Skinner had already become familiar as the author of several carefully stated research reports. During the five years as a National Research Council Fellow and as a junior member of the Harvard Society of Fellows, Skinner had not only researched deeply but had conscientiously published. He was not destined to perish either professionally or personally, and in 1936 he married Yvonne Blue, an English major from the University of Chicago, who set the occasion for, and duly reinforced, further extensions of his literary interests.

By the fall of 1941 the thirty-seven-year-old psychologist began a final draft of the book which was eventually to be called, laconically enough but (to traditionalists) threateningly, *Verbal Behavior*.

Because of World War II, however, and other intervening activities connected with the war, the work was delayed and did not appear as a book until 1957. Not surprisingly, Skinner's contribution to the war effort was made in his laboratory, where, for example, he succeeded in designing and testing missiles guided by pigeons.

Skinner assumed that "our side" must win although he also went on experimenting with paranational behavior. One such project, which is still anathema to humanists, resulted in the invention of a device for controlling the environment of an infant. The local occasion for the invention was the birth of a second child in the Skinner family. Some help with rearing the infant was needed. The result was a "baby box," or more properly called "air crib," which is a sophisticated version of the first Skinner box designed as an environment for a rat's education. The temperature and other important features of the infant's environment are controlled sensibly to safeguard the child's health; nevertheless, the air crib still seems too mechanical to most parents.

Although Skinner's device for ordering the all too often chaotic environment of an infant was adapted to human needs rather than to those of rodents, it does deny the child the right to experience all the slings and arrows of those outrageous fortunes humans have come to expect. Pigeons, unlike children, have often been encouraged—even by humanists—to potentiate their talents in a controlled environment. It is more than merely amusing that Skinner was able to teach pigeons not only to guide missiles but also to play a decent game of ping pong. (Perhaps, of course, neither humans nor pigeons should spend time in such meretricious activities as playing war or other games.) The fact that Skinner was aware of the controversial aspects of his work, in the laboratory as well as on campus and at home, certainly helped motivate the writing of *Walden Two* at this time. The novel is an attempt to communicate with nonspecialists and a serious effort to better the world.

One night in 1945 at a party in Minneapolis, Skinner expressed regret over the fact that after the war many servicemen would probably lose their idealism. In answer to one guest's request for a program that would support the youths' "crusading spirit" Skinner outlined the "Good Life" that could be achieved by adopting an experimental attitude toward social problems. The occasion led to the writing of *Walden Two* (1948) as a more nearly complete answer to the question. This work, which has become a popular handbook of behaviorism, was written in just seven weeks, and its fate at first seemed uncertain, for it was often read as a dystopia.[12] Over the years, however, Skinner has accepted considerable responsibility for reinforcing a minority enthusiasm for a good life. After the war, as Skinner continued to accelerate his research, his significance also increased, and he was soon confronted by the nuisances as well as the benefits of success.

IX   Changing the Answers

In 1945 Skinner served briefly as chairman of his department at Indiana University. His lack of enthusiasm for administrative details led to his shortly thereafter abandoning that particular distraction. "American Behaviorism" (sometimes capitalized when qualified nationally as well as conceived pejoratively) was now ready to be defined and defended. A conference at Indiana University in the spring of 1946 is a convenient birthdate for the new psychology. The event proved to be only the first of a sturdy series of annual meetings underwritten by Skinner and his friend and colleague Fred Keller, who with W. N. Schoenfeld was promoting behavioral science at Columbia University and enthusiastically using Skinner's *The Behavior of Organisms* as a textbook.

The annual conferences on "The Experimental Analysis of Behavior" eventually became a "division" of the American Psychological Association and generated in 1958 its own professional periodical, *Journal of the Experimental Analysis of Behavior*, the first issue of which defined the significant difference between other psychologies and Skinner's. What Keller called a "dangerous quip" in the page-one article in the new journal[13] was not without ominous overtones. "Facts" in psychology had become so ephemeral because of basic disagreements about content and method that Keller's anxiety was aroused one day when he overheard an assistant in the lab commenting on the futility of a student's consulting files of old examinations. The assistant admitted that the same questions were used over and over again, "but we change the answers."

Keller reports that he realized that "changing answers was, in truth, a sign of good health in any course of study." Obviously Keller and other "Skinnerians" were also beginning to change the questions. For example, to measure the "strength of the reflex" in conditioning they were using rates rather than quantities. Also, they began to translate *why* questions into *how* questions, preferring operational terms to philosophical abstractions.

With an elegant simplicity that is still misunderstood even by many psychologists, Skinner began carefully to distinguish between correlations and cause-and-effect sequences. His discovery that certain events in one's environment literally only set the occasion for, rather than cause, certain responses expanded the definition of conditioned behavior to include so-called voluntary acts. When Skinner decided to return to Harvard in 1948, presumably he was behaving predictably. The "occasion" was his delivery in Cambridge of the William James Lectures, in which he used material later to be expanded into the book *Verbal Behavior*. He apparently impressed the proper people, for his return to Harvard as lecturer was soon followed by the offer of a professorship. The comparatively young man felt somewhat triumphant, one imagines, at becoming a permanent member of the department which had not long before rejected his dissertation.

Skinner remembers his first teaching year at Harvard as not an easy time. Many students were attracted to Skinner's offerings, liked the phrase "human behavior," but did not anticipate Skinnerian rigor in an area still trailing clouds of philosophical speculations. To help such students Skinner wrote *Science and Human Behavior* (1953), a more technical and thus less popular treatment of the ideas projected in *Walden Two*. Meanwhile Skinner continued his own research program as the Harvard students began, presumably, to be more cautious in their enthusiasm for "psych courses" taught by "that fellow Skinner," who was reputed to be a kind of demon or dehumanized computer in his insistence on facts.

X *Success*

During the next several years Skinner worked with Charles Ferster, refining and varying the experimental contingencies in the environment of pigeons. The result was a book with more than 900 figures appropriately called *Schedules of Reinforcement* (1957). This work set paradigms and defined parameters for much subsequent experimentation as Skinner's dedicated students began to accelerate their own research, adding to the sophistication of the operant-conditioning model by identifying more and more subtle relationships between occasions, reinforcements, and strength of learning. Indeed, it began to seem that Skinner's original heresy was being embraced by enough followers to suggest an analogy with Satan's rebellion against Authority, a *non-serviam* act in which one third of the angels followed the Arch Rebel into a hopeless yet valiant war against that Omnipotence which had already decreed the damnation of the rebels. In a word, there began to be "Skinnerians": psychologists who, on the basis of certain evidence, had apparently freely renounced freedom in the name of science to follow their leader, a bold fellow, who had rebelled against knowledge not based on experimentation. The issue was finely drawn. That all was well in Heaven when Satan rebelled is axiomatic to the orthodox. That Satan was heroic in asking for debate and dialectic instead of hymn singing and praising God is equally axiomatic to the heretics. Eventually, of course, Satan's followers lost themselves in mazes of philosophical abstractions. Would Skinner's rebellion also flounder in nit-picking and internecine jealousies? Would it be able to survive its increasing sophistication? Time is still of the essence, but in any event Skinner personally survived his own significance, and his vision, absurdly heroic as it may be, has also survived some revision. He always did know the difference between pigeons and poets but had often been too busy with the former to tell the latter. Skinnerians began to look at humans more closely.

At Minnesota, Skinner and his co-worker W. T. Heron had introduced drugs into their subjects' internal environments. They were aware of the controversial new uses of drugs as sacraments and the possible therapeutic effects of altering the body's chemistry, but their experiments were relatively austere as they concentrated on correlations between observable behavior and controllable aspects of the environment. The possibility of altering the behavior of psychotics, for example, in the direction of nonpsychotic behavior without resorting to Freudian fictions about ids and icebergs seemed very good.

Pavlovian or instrumental reconditioning was an inadequate method for altering behavior generally considered voluntary or cognitive. Whether Skinner succeeded in curing patients remains moot only insofar as the definition of "cure" goes. Certainly by reconditioning patients operantly he did succeed in producing a facsimile of reasonable behavior in which patients were taught to get to work. That "work" may be only the insertion of tokens into a machine which then ejects a rather simple meal but the patients began to cope with reality—anyone's rule-of-thumb definition of sanity. Depth psychologists, such as Dr. R. D. Laing, have belittled mere modifications of the *overt* behavior of psychotics as not coming to terms with anxiety. Skinnerians defend their kind of therapy, on the other hand, as the most efficient way to change people. If the sane want sanely to help the insane become sane, in all good faith they must teach the insane to behave more and more as the sane do. In general, orthodox Skinnerians are convinced that talk-it-out therapy, pleasant as it may be at the time for a lonely patient, is relatively ineffective in teaching a person how to behave *as if* he were well. That *as if* is the sole criterion a nonspeculative behaviorist needs. Einstein, for example, behaved *as if* he were a brilliant scientist—and did it very well. Other people alleged to be brilliant have *done* nothing significant. To Skinner, in full possession of his new psychology, *doing* became the only test of whether anything can be done. He began to see the *how* of living more clearly as time passed, thus alienating philosophers and other theorists for whom the *why* came first.

From conditioning psychotics and retardates to educating so-called normal humans is not a giant step for behaviorists, so inevitably Skinner became interested in ways of improving the education not only of rats, pigeons, and "normal" grown-ups but also of children. Because the full repertory of skills his animal subjects were physically capable of learning had never before been potentiated in their natural environments, no one except a few bird trainers, for example, had suspected how clever pigeons—even ordinary ones—could be, and only a few rat fanciers and many more dog lovers had educated their pets. Skinner taught pigeons to play ping pong, to bowl, and to pilot missiles long before he realized that his own children were being deprived of a constructive education. In fact, not until November 11, 1953, when as a "Visiting Father" he attended an arithmetic class, did he see what was happening. With the acute perception he had perfected in laboratories Skinner suddenly *looked* carefully at what the teacher was actually doing. He quickly drew some conclusions: "Here were twenty extremely valuable organisms. Through no fault of her own the teacher was violating almost everything we knew about the learning process."[14]

So, without further fuss the Skinner-organism, trained to minimize theory, began to analyze those contingencies of reinforcement which could be significant in a technology of education. Because he seemed to be down-grading students into subjects and teachers into machines, Skinner predictably again aroused hostility. Although humanists have always claimed teaching is a mysterious art and thus *real* learning is not merely a mechanical event, Skinner designed and advocated "teaching machines," which he first demonstrated at a conference at the University of Pittsburgh in 1954. Shortly thereafter, Skinner notes, he found himself "caught up in the teaching machine movement."[15] Collaborating with James G. Holland, Skinner explored the potentials of programmed instruction and in due time published the results of his experiments.

XI   *Fame and Infamy*

As Skinner's interests progressed from rats-in-boxes through babies-in-cribs to children-in-schools he appeared more and more threatening to more and more vested interests, including sincere humanists and religious. For Skinner, his controversial "discoveries" were simple facts not known until he or his followers had established them. His consistent and relentless search for "new" truths increasingly antagonized traditionalists. It was well enough, they rationalized, when Skinner kept to his rats and pigeons, even to his looneys and dumb kids, but now that he is working on us and wants to change everything, we must resist. In contrast, however, to such predictable hostility, a growing awareness of B. F. Skinner's greatness began to awe professional colleagues, even those who heartily disagreed with him. In 1958 the American Psychological Association had awarded Skinner their Distinguished Scientific Contribution Award. The citation acknowledges Skinner's eminence and identifies his uniqueness, calling him "an imaginative and creative scientist, characterized by great objectivity in scientific matters and by warmth and enthusiasm in personal contacts." The citation specifies his significance as a behaviorist who "has challenged alternative analyses of behavior, insisting that description take precedence over hypotheses." It also specifies his methods: "By careful control of experimental conditions, he has produced data which are relatively free from fortuitous variation. Despite his antitheoretical position, he is considered an important systematist and has developed a self-consistent description of behavior which has greatly increased our ability to predict and control the behavior of organisms from rat to man. . . ."[16]

Skinner's professional concerns during the busy years following this important recognition became more and more expansive as he boldly began to attack the *social* sciences with reference not only to their methods but also to their goals. He began also to take the vision he projected in *Walden Two* as seriously as enthusiastic youths might once have wished—but with a difference. He saw that it was time not to join a commune but to search out the "common principles" shared by economics, government, and religion with psychology, linguistics, psychotherapy, and education—in order to save the world! This broader concern, of course, also attracted broader resistance from those he was trying to make admit their own wrongness. The result was an increase in passion on both sides, so that beginning in the 1960s and continuing on into the 1970s Skinner emerges more and more as the heroic defender of his faith.

CHAPTER 2

The Nadir of Ignominy or Zenith of Glory?

F ROM time to time gentle men as well as madmen have drawn up specifications for happiness this side of Heaven but most of their utopias have been just that—impractical visions justifiably dismissed as too idealistic to be taken seriously. Unlike earlier blueprints for a brave new world Skinner's invitation to the Good Life outlined in his novel *Walden Two* has set the occasion for serious experiments led by questing youths such as Skinner invented in his story. Less fictitious specifications for improving society appear in Skinner's later books. To the nonspecialist, however, the novel is still the most accessible statement of the essence of Skinnerism. It is thus an appropriate introduction to a survey of Skinner's significance as a scientist and a measure of his potential leadership. Nadir of ignominy or zenith of glory, *Walden Two* today stimulates even more viable debate than when it was published in 1948. The verdict is by no means unanimous on any side, even among those who believe in the possibility of improving life here and now. In fact, a clear and vociferous majority of critics have damned the work as vicious and demeaning without thoughtful evidence. One criticism may here speak for legions. Referring to Skinner's projection of an engineered community, the authors of a recent survey of "quests for utopia" cite the usual charge against Skinner that he does not distinguish between humans and pigeons: "[In *Walden Two*] we have descended from the heights of confidence in man's capacities and noble aspirations for his progressive betterment to a nadir of ignominy in which he is placed on a par with pigeons."[1] Defenders of the work, on the other hand, have been less articulate and more inclined to *test* the vision than debate its merits—as, of course, behaviorists should.

In another context *Walden Two* is much more innocent, partly because of the relative literary ingenuousness of the author and the consequent failure of the book to achieve Tolstoian greatness, and partly because Skinner really meant well when he wrote it, possibly more simply well than he did later when he invited humanity to go beyond its freedom and dignity in search of means to survive. The story line of *Walden Two*, however, and the characterizations are quite adequate to its author's purpose. Although the style is neat and parsimonious—really deceptively clean writing—the work has not attracted the attention of literary critics who read and praise Thomas More's *Utopia* and Philip Sidney's *Arcadia*, for example, without approving of any of the *ideas* in either work. *Walden Two* is usually read for its ideas, and so clearly are those ideas presented that any hostile philosopher can find plenty of grist to grind in his humanistic mill. In a real sense, then, *Walden Two* has been a success precisely because of its failure. It is a work well worth analyzing and evaluating.

I   *The Story Is the Thing*

Storytelling is not an inappropriate modality for a scientist to ex-periment with, for a story projects a controlled universe. The par-ticular "one day" on which a story begins is followed by a series of events which, being both subsequent and consequent, play changes on predictability just as intricately varied schedules of reinforce-ment do in laboratory experiments. Besides, stories are well-tried devices to catch the conscience of guilty readers.

Skinner's novel begins just after World War II with the appearance of two young men in the office of Professor Burris, a bachelor psychologist. The young men are disaffected by peace and have come to inquire about Professor Burris' former interest in a community that was to be built "with the benefit of modern techniques" by "a queer duck" whom he had known, named Frazier, in graduate school.[2] As a result, Burris writes to Frazier, and eventually receives an invitation to visit a place optimistically called "Walden Two." Burris and Burris' colleague, Professor Augustine Castle of the Philosophy Department, and the two young men and their girl friends immediately set out for the promised land.

The location of Walden Two is only vaguely indicated but the group makes no perilous journey across mountains or into the bowels of the earth. Instead, they ride on a public bus down a road just off a highway, cross over a small bridge, and pass through fertile farmland. When Frazier himself meets the bus, they all proceed to Walden Two by station wagon. A nondescript, middle-aged contemporary of Burris and Castle, Frazier is friendly although his glance is described as "intensely searching" (10).

Frazier explains that Walden Two is located on several farms bought for overdue taxes. Enthusiastically he points to certain benefits of scientific controls, such as sheep conditioned not to stray from their pasture, the wonderfully clear water in the bathing pond, and the cooperative housing arrangements designed to minimize the tyranny of unpredictable weather. As the group enters a long passageway conveniently cut up into "alcoves" where friends can meet, Burris notices that although the pictures on one of the windowless walls are unfamiliar they are "extraordinarily good" (20). Apparently art as such is not engineered. Tea time, however, has been subjected to an experimental approach. The tea is drunk from glasses which can be carried like little pails, eliminating the need for cups and saucers. The other dishes are all uniformly square: "a nice little job in domestic engineering" (22).

Under questioning, Frazier carefully distinguishes between Thoreau's Walden and his own. Unlike the original Walden, the second Walden provides more than basic subsistence. Neither solitude nor simplicity is necessarily desirable, Frazier points out. After a few sample experiences with the gentle life in Walden Two, the group is escorted by Frazier through a long corridor along both sides of which are arranged libraries and lounges and all of which are occupied by residents during the predinner time. Frazier stresses the fact that Walden Two has overcome the evils of institutionalizing by encouraging staggered schedules and independence from routines. For example, although the theater holds no more than two hundred people, all performances, including concerts, are repeated when necessary; thus the size of each audience is kept comfortably small.

That evening Frazier describes their four-hour working day and the flexible pay scale based on a credit system of evaluating a job "in terms of the willingness of the members to undertake it" (41). He also outlines other unusual features of the government, such as the emphasis on Planners and Managers. These titles are not considered honorific. The nonexistence of leisure classes, a situation which allegedly eliminates personal jealousy, arouses suspicion in the visiting philosopher, Professor Castle, who interprets the classless society as outlawing "personal freedom." Frazier, however, enthusiastically defends the cooperative labor system of Walden Two as a fact and not a theory. He also announces that tomorrow he expects from each of the guests a "full day's work" (52).

The guests' assignments, however, turn out to be pleasantly diverting and take up only a few morning hours. After lunch the visitors inspect the food lockers, a dairy farm, and various shops, where people do not seem to be working very hard. Later that evening Burris is impressed with the abundance and variety of recreational events available to the members, such as meetings, concerts, and parties. Frazier explains that thanks to cultural engineering, Walden Two has achieved a veritable Golden Age.

After attending a concert, a fifty-minute version of the Bach *B Minor Mass,* the two young couples go off to a dance while Burris remains alone to meditate. He now dares to ask himself: "*Why not? Why not?*" (76). His fantasies begin to merge with the realities he is observing, and although he tries to stiffen his resistance, he does so only because he feels the increased power of seduction. After all, he has been trained to distrust enthusiasms and quick conversions.

The next morning is given over to observing the children in an out-of-doors school. As the visitors note the apparent well-being of the infants in the Lower Nursery, Frazier explains how the children are taught to tolerate frustration by being gradually exposed to annoying stimuli. After showing the visitors other examples of how education has benefited from behavioral engineering, Frazier admits that the family has been deliberately attenuated. The community at large has replaced the family economically, socially, and psychologically. Countering Professor Castle's concern over the absence of mother-love, Frazier explains: "We go in for father love, too—for everybody's love—community love, if you wish" (80).

After dinner that night Frazier takes the group to a pleasant roof top. As twilight turns to night, Frazier outlines his concept of the Good Life. Because Walden Two is scientifically engineered and thus is unsentimental and nonidealistic, it promotes good health, minimum labor, creative recreation, satisfying personal relationships, and plenty of simple relaxation and rest. Burris is impressed, and later he walks alone in the garden, smoking and thinking about all he has seen and heard.

II *Burris Thinks*

In ordinary novels, and particularly in utopian novels, characters often do a lot of thinking, for characters in serious fiction must appear to be free to make choices or the story lacks dramatic tension. Although after making critical choices they are compelled by the novelist to suffer the consequences—or more happily, to reap the benefits—the characters must seem to act like real people. In the behavioral scientist's universe, however, degrees of freedom are limited, if not nonexistent. The flow of events in the scientist's real world is theoretically impervious to individual will. Thus Burris' awareness of the effect on him of the observations he has been making in Walden Two poses a problem for Skinner-as-novelist.

When Steve later asks Burris for his opinion of Walden Two, Burris answers ambiguously that he "thinks" Frazier is telling the truth. Burris supposedly means that he is willing to believe Frazier. Actually, of course, he has been made to appear to believe him by the novelist who created him, but the character does not, obviously, admit he is only a character. (He could also deliberately be telling a lie!) The reader of the novel has so far, however, been invited by the novelist to find Burris' credulousness as reliable as Castle's skepticism; that is, both are projected as moral beings reacting honestly to the evidence. At this point the novelist has necessarily embraced the logic of fiction rather than the logic of behavioral science for the sake of a dramatic moment. When Steve tells Burris that he and Mary have "decided" to stay in Walden Two, Burris' emotional reaction is idiomatic to fiction rather than scientifically sound. Behaviorally speaking, no one is freely deciding anything. Burris' apparent flaw is openness to demonstration of fact; however, since this is no Greek drama the flaw does not lead to tragedy. Instead, Burris easily moves toward Skinner's pleasant fate for him, which is happiness without hubris. Readers trained to correlate flaws with tragic endings would inevitably lament Burris' conversion, saying in effect: "I'd rather be dead than end up in Walden Two." Conditioned to fear man's capacity to be convinced, such readers want to warn Burris at this point to beware, for no one has the right to find happiness so easily. Moral beings must earn happiness with anguish, at least with enough anguish to wipe out the guilt of being happy.

In any event, the next morning Castle announces that "the whole thing's a hoax." In a crescendo of indignation he explodes: "It's nothing more or less than personal magnetism. The Führer principle. He's got these people hypnotized. Makes them work like sin. Keeps them smiling for the sake of appearances" (154). Nevertheless, despite Castle's objections, one of the young men and his girl have decided to join Walden Two, and Frazier is triumphant. More cautiously than ever, therefore, Burris begins early that afternoon systematically to check his first impressions of the community. He visits a series of the "stages" and observes the doings of the people there. He also observes the activities of the people outdoors. All seem "engaged in some apparently profitable or enjoyable activity" (179). He happens upon a group making music together. Frazier is at the piano in a serious but not grim performance of the first movement of the Schumann Piano Quintet. Although an amateur, Frazier clearly shows his enjoyment in his playing.

Continuing his investigation, Burris acknowledges to himself his objective. He is searching for some flaw in the Good Life. His short conversation with Mrs. Olson, a middle-aged pastry cook and the kind of person Burris suspected might be bored in Walden Two, is decisive. Apparently Mrs. Olson is also unselfconsciously happy. She has no problems. Furthermore, her contentment is not a function of merely "keeping busy." In fact she insists that she hasn't been busy in years.

That afternoon the increasingly hostile Castle hurls his final charge at Frazier: "I accuse you of one of the most diabolical machinations in the history of mankind!" (209). For hours the founder of Walden Two answers in detail the philosopher's accusations of the prevalence of despotism, dictatorship, and totalitarianism in the community. Distinguishing between "control" and "force," Frazier explains the use of positive reinforcement in getting results. He passionately defends the reality and virtue of a science of human behavior and distinguishes between the philosophical defense of freedom and the semantic abuses of the concept. Dramatically, in support of his thesis, he cites Jesus' accidental discovery of the principle which behavioral science later experimentally verified: to love one's enemies is positively reinforcing.

In the climax moment Frazier takes Burris aside and tempts him with an offer of much work still to be done in Walden Two. He announces, with no apparent awareness of irony, that one "must never be free of that feverish urge to push forward which is the saving grace of mankind" (241). Then he leads Burris to a ledge overlooking the community from which they can observe, with the help of a pocket telescope Frazier always carries, the doings of the Walden people. Half humorously Burris accuses Frazier of thinking he is

God. When Frazier seems to admit it, Burris is shocked. Frazier quickly explains, however, that he is really less a dictator than God is. Frazier grandly dismisses the logical problem of how he came freely to decide that decision making is not a free act. Burris seems satisfied with the high-handed resolution of the impasse.

After lunch all visitors except the young couple who have decided to stay leave Walden Two. On the bus Burris does not sit with Castle; and when back in the city Castle continues to rant against Frazier and his utopian experiment, Burris leaves him, finds a small park in which he can "think." He decides that he will walk back to Walden Two as a pilgrim and join. In the station he had bought a copy of Thoreau's *Walden*—a "good omen," he calls it. Opening his copy of *Walden* to the last page, he reads Thoreau's concluding paragraph. The mysticism had once offended him. Now, however, he understands what Thoreau meant when he wrote: "The light which puts out our eyes is darkness to us. Only that day dawns to which we are awake. There is more day to dawn. The sun is but a morning-star" (262).

In an epiloguelike final chapter the novelist jumps ahead in time. As part of his contribution as a new member, Burris is writing the story of his decision to join Walden Two. Burris has suggested ending the story with the quotation from Thoreau but Frazier advises him to include the final details, noting that "some fool professor is going to assign your book as outside reading in a course in political science" (263). After Frazier proposes several other possible but untrue endings in which Burris never reached Walden Two, Burris settles for the account of his three-day walk back to the happy place, which is the true ending. As he approached Walden Two he was met by his former student, who had been watching for him because the omniscient Frazier had known all along that Burris would return.

III   Walden Two *As Literature*

Philosophically, literature is strategy. In Skinnerian terms, the imaginative writer is nonsensible in that his strategy is aimed at increasing resistance to extinction of the ultimately futile habit of pressing levers or some other action for few tangible rewards. The imaginative writer uses tricks to keep the reader reading, such as incantations. He reaches for the sun, the moon, and the stars without any real hope of touching them. In the end his reader is rewarded with illusions alone. Words are not pellets of food, but apparently they can be quite reinforcing even when not true.

In *Walden Two* Skinner relinquished many of the conventional strategies of literature in favor of stating facts as he stressed experimentally verifiable mechanisms of control over human behavior. Thus in his fictitious community the odds are *with* sensible men rather than *against* them, an unusual situation for dramatic literature. Unavoidably Skinner put himself in double jeopardy. As a scientist he appears nonsensible in that he extrapolates beyond reality in giving us a vision, and as a novelist he is all-too-sensible in that his characters make few heroic leaps; that is, they generally behave predictably as a function of their heredity and experience. Frazier and Burris, being products of a good heredity and an enlightened environment, finally respond reasonably and with a minimum of suffering. To literary critics trained to search for Dostoeveskian anguish, the "action" in *Walden Two* seems superficial and even dull.

Many truisms insist upon the inevitability of ambivalence and paradox in life. Thus, although man's highest good may be personal happiness, man is supposed to suffer for that happiness. The so-called well-adjusted man, stranded midway between his longing for a better life and his fear of a worse life, has been encouraged to settle for a present in which he is praised for his dreams of bettering himself. At the same time he is rewarded for his failure to yield to despair at not being able to better himself, all the while seeking congratulations on his anguished awareness of the complexity of it all. Evil has been justified as the underside of good. Good costs, evil pays. Scores of proverbs describe the paradox, yet most men do not embrace evil willingly. That black clouds are redeemed by silver linings is a rationalization *after* the fact. Although yesterday's rationalizations easily become today's clichés, they *need* not become tomorrow's laws. Literature is contrived to be either a temporary solution (escape) or a final resolution (catharsis). Nobody really *believes* in a story except while being manipulated by the artful storyteller. A story is, by definition and in fact, fictitious. As such one expects it to be a distortion of reality.

Dreams of pure, unpaid-for happiness have frequently turned up as utopian projections, as "nowheres" invented by writers-turned-philosophers or philosophers-turned-writers. Most of these visions are divisible into positive and negative—pleasant dreams of perpetual happiness-remaining-sweet or nightmares of perpetual happiness-turning-sour. Orwell's *1984* is a nightmare projection. Butler's *Erewhon* is a pleasant-dream projection. Neither one was meant to be as real as reality. Neither one projects a universe as threatening or as reassuring as reality. Both *1984* and *Erewhon* arouse illusory hopes and false fears. A real fear, as of a present, attacking bear, is easily distinguishable from Orwell's warning of what-might-happen-if we-are-not-wise; and a real pleasure, such as a sexual orgasm, is equally easily distinguishable from a delight in Butler's vision of what-could-happen-if-we-were-wise.

"Nowhere" spelled backward (actually slightly mispelled) is "Erewhon," the locale Samuel Butler chose for his vision of social perfection. This backward version of nowhere is not, however, in fact somewhere, for Butler's dream of what-could-be implies a low probability of attainment. We could never be wise enough. The reversed spelling is only a gimmick, and the place remains a never-never land.

Although still incredible, the nowhere which has the higher probability of becoming is the antiutopia, or dystopia, as it is sometimes called. Here the double negative, the antinowhereness, suggests the horror of something highly probable someday. Orwell's *1984* and Huxley's *Brave New World* are famous examples of dystopias, and the differences between the two projections are only incidental. Both writers intended to warn humanity against totalitarianism and technologically created contentment. Man is losing his freedom, they announced. Someday only "savages" will be allowed to make choices. The champions of freedom—before Skinner—never allowed their protagonists freely to reject freedom. Everyone in a free country is taught to defend "freedom" even at the cost of freedom. (Skinner later probed this paradox, trying to avoid jingoism.)

Skinner's *Walden Two* minimizes rhetorical appeals to "save" anything. For its time it is a precise, unambiguous vision of pleasant people doing pleasant things. Ironically enough, however, it is misread as antiutopian by those who reject experimental methods in particular and behavioral science in general as means to Truth. The bias, of course, blinds such readers to the pleasantness which Skinner projects. Readers see the author as unreliable, as downright untruthful, or even as a villain out to swindle them, and thus they must inevitably conclude that Skinner's vision of happiness is evil precisely *because* of all the promised happiness, which they redefine in their own terms as boredom, blandness, and sterility.

Such a response is obviously an egregious misreading of the work. Those who for various reasons are terrified by the implications reject Skinner's vision even as a vision and then go on to distort even his simplest assertions, compounding misunderstandings.

Skinner is not Frazier nor is he Burris. If anything, he has divided himself between the two. In the dramatic context of the story Frazier's intense enthusiasm is too unscientific and too subjective. He is set up as not entirely trustworthy. His emotional endorsement of behavioral engineering calls forth counterenthusiasms from the philosopher Castle, who represents the status quo and a muddled but honest resistance to brainwashing and propaganda. Skinner's characters were devised by the story-teller to explicate and defend a gradient of attitudes and to represent a range from lies to objective facts. Frazier's pride in what behavioral engineering has accomplished in the community makes him seem arrogant. Skinner at that time was not necessarily equally arrogant. When Frazier is sure of his facts nothing penetrates his assurance. Frazier is neither modest nor compassionate. He is the kind of intellectual who arouses hostility in other intellectuals as well as in less sophisticated observers. His coolness extends to not contradicting even effusive compliments. If he has a so-called personality problem, it is that he has identified himself as a genius in a culture which is reluctant to accept such self-evaluation. The democratic game calls for modest, self-deprecatory gestures, no matter how insincere they may be. Although one of the traits of genius logically should be its ability to identify itself, Frazier's thrust toward greatness might be considered insane outside Walden Two. Inside Walden Two he is relatively well adjusted. After all, the place *is* his own dream projection, possibly a topological map of his own madness.

It doesn't take much subtlety to detect Skinner observing some aspects of himself as he created Frazier. When Frazier reminds Burris that Frazier is not himself a product of Walden Two and thus Burris should not look for perfection in him, Skinner is possibly apologizing for certain personal traits of his own. Frazier advises Burris: "You can safely leave me out. Forget me and turn your face on heaven" (208).

Heaven is everyone's destination. Burris has no reason not to accept the offer. A bachelor, he is free from family responsibilities; yet he is not a hermit. He has been successful as a teacher, although mostly inadvertently; that is, his students remember him best for his digressions. After the war, in which he "had assumed an appropriate sense of social responsibility, in spite of a contrary inclination of long standing," he could not return to old patterns and old ways of getting by. "My new interest in social problems," he explains in the opening of the narrative, "and my good will appeared to have exactly no effect whatsoever upon society. I could not see that they were of the slightest value to anyone. Yet I continued to pay for them day after day with a sustained feeling of frustration and depression" (3).

Burris' willingness to go see plus his good-natured acceptance of the ironic results of teaching are evidence of intelligence. Skinner neither flattered himself as he drew up the specifications for Frazier nor understated his own virtues as he designed Burris. Only pedants, not real teachers, and only pseudoscholars, not searchers after truth, are without doubt and anxiety in the real world. Despair over what uses venal men make of their research has frequently tempered scientists' enthusiasm for Science.

Although as narrator Burris does not spell out all of his disaffection, Skinner has firmly made Burris a highly probable convert to Frazier's program. He is the kind of troubled fellow who is honest with himself. Just before he capitulates he admits that he had wanted to find something wrong. As a trained scientist he is addicted to objectivity but is aware of the compulsion and has tempered it with other concerns. He reacts intensely to music, particularly to the "Kyrie Eleison" from the Bach *Mass*. His hunger for the Good Life is neither neurotic nor simplistic, and he is certainly not illiterate. His conversion to Walden Two is meant to be a breakthrough rather than a retreat. True, he has had problems he is glad to leave behind, but he is not simply fleeing the real world. Veteran teachers readily sympathize with his comment on his way back to Walden Two. He realizes he is glad to leave the university. "It would be a pleasure," he admits, "not to worry about being too obscure for the dull, too obvious for the bright, or unfair to those who were taking the course for practical purposes" (265).

IV *The Good Life*

In *Walden Two*, science makes an unequivocal offer. As the discoveries of experimental psychology are "engineered" to achieve the so-called Good Life, the rejection of traditional freedom becomes logically necessary. "You can't have a science about a subject matter which hops about capriciously," Skinner has often asserted. The result of the rejection of freedom, however, is not necessarily negative. Man is not asked to relinquish his good dreams. The scientists in *Walden Two* have dispensed with the traditional trial-and-error kind of freedom because it is ineffective in achieving any goal. Efficiency in achieving a given goal is demonstrably related to the systematic use of positive reinforcements. Hit-and-miss attempts to get what one wants give way to better methods for increasing the probability of desirable behavior. Positive reinforcement, which in most cases is pleasantly similar to love, works; and because it works, it controls. Anyway, effectiveness is always the logical criterion of success. Thus sadly enough, even Christians and other advocates of the power of love may well fear the logic of *Walden Two*. If wars can be won with love instead of with bullets, then warriors ought also to adopt this effective weapon, for love is totally effective. What price sacrifice when deprivation leads to aggrandizement!

That men's reflexes can be conditioned is admitted by even the most ardent of humanists. The objection is to the assertion that voluntary behavior is also conditioned. The compromise, advocated by Roman Catholic psychologists, for example, is to believe that a phrase like "partly determined" has a meaning. Obviously *any* part-not-determined in man, no matter how small or reticent, could disarm and discredit absolute determinism by doing capricious things. Even a soul may be determined to be saved—or lost. Determinism, however, is not logically qualifiable without becoming "indeterminism" just as freedom cannot survive restraints without introducing paradoxes. It seems that most humanists are "determined" to avoid determinism at all costs, including the cost of a paradox or two. The result is a semantic nightmare—to behavioral scientists, at least. Theologians are, of course, positively reinforced for bending facts. The simplicity of putting the issue to a test does not appeal to specialists in vested jargons, but if man sometimes yields to conditioning and sometimes resists conditioning, then the scientist eventually must ascertain when man does yield and when he does not yield. No fact should ever disconcert a scientist, even if the fact should turn out to be that facts are not stable entities.

Obviously Skinner's Walden Two is not a religious community in the usual meaning of the word "religious." Burris, however, at the point of "conversion," identifies certain aspects of the program as religious, using the term loosely. Burris sees the experiment as "a religious movement freed of any dallying with the supernatural and inspired by a determination to build heaven on earth" (256). Those who believe religious value can exist without revelation would find Walden Two in that respect not an impossible dream, but those who subscribe only to revealed truths would find life in Walden Two incompatible with their religious commitment. Thus the debate must be waged in other terms; for behavioral science, whatever evil it may represent, is not a *cause* of nonbelief in God.

The goal in Walden Two is to "make every man a brave man" (93). Yet there are no stadiums, no tournaments, and no hero-worshippers because there is no need for heroes. Athletic persons who dive gracefully or pole-vault extraordinarily are appreciated, but there are no boxing or wrestling matches. Everyone in the community is encouraged to try his skills in the arts and crafts. There are rooms in Walden Two in which to display paintings and to make music, and there is always plenty of time. To the objection that great works of art are motivated only by the kind of anguish which Walden Two has eliminated, Frazier answers: "Not many works of art can be traced to the lack of satisfaction of the basic needs" (103). When Burris makes his survey of Walden Two just before capitulating, he says of the paintings and sculpture he sees: "Nothing seemed to be merely on display" (127). Art in the sense of expressing by doing is an integral part of the Good Life in Walden Two. Just how great such art could become may be questionable, but it is possible that the purpose of art is to make art unnecessary. When life itself attains the style art is supposed to give life, the need for art would certainly decline. By the same token, however, if the need for art as escape from frustration disappeared, art forms could begin to express themselves in all activities.

When there is no need to placate anxiety by imitating temples and palaces, good architecture is reducible to efficient engineering. In general, as one would expect, all the buildings in Walden are functional; that is, they have been designed to facilitate playing and working. Built of low-cost material they appear at first to outsiders as unpleasantly institutionalized. The smallness, alikeness, and stripped-down appearance of the living rooms is not, however, a disagreeable quality to those members of the community who no longer have any need to express themselves via idiosyncratic interior decor. At the same time Frazier makes it clear that every person's room is his own castle.

"Cultural engineering" is not a pejorative expression in Walden Two. Of necessity, then, there are Managers and Planners such as a

Kitchen Manager, Social Manager, Political Manager, Legal
Manager, Manager of Marriages, Manager of Public Relations,
Manager of Cultural Behavior, Manager of Personal Behavior, and
the various Managers of Food, Health, Plays, Art, Dentistry, Supply, Labor, Education (Advanced and Elementary). The titles of
Managers are distributed so liberally about the community that
they lose their original awesomeness. Although there are only six
Planners, they are always chosen by the many Managers. When a
replacement is needed, the Managers supply the Board of Planners
with two names from which the Board selects one. The members of
the community, however, do not vote directly for either Planners or
Managers, and thus there is no pretense that Walden Two is a
democracy.

Since there are no heroes and no rewards for heroic action,
neither Planners nor Managers are concerned about status or
acclaim. Nevertheless, the absence of elections remains the most
controversial aspect of the planning-managing and the planned-
managed relationships in Walden Two. When the planned and
managed are allowed to elect their planners and their managers
directly as their representatives, there is an apparent safeguard
against despotism and other forms of usurped power. In Walden
Two, however, there is no power to usurp. Traditional symbols of
power, such as gems and capital wealth, are supplanted by units of
positive reinforcement. Actually, Walden Two is frankly projected
as a limited sort of despotism. Of course, the nature of the limitation
is what counts. Enlightened planners plan and informed managers
manage as they check one another. The people know what they
want, from the simple Mrs. Olson to the intellectuals and research
scientists. They want time to work and freedom from the need to
defend freedom with violence. Their freedom may be precarious
anywhere other than in a story, but here they gain freedom by
renouncing it.

V   A Reasonable Guess

In 1945, when Skinner wrote *Walden Two*, he was only hazard-
ing a reasonable guess, according to his own statement later. In
1967 a group of enthusiasts began to test Skinner's blueprint for the
Good Life in a living experiment in Twin Oaks, Virginia. The report
of that experiment written in 1972 by Kathleen Kinkade, one of the
founders, stresses both the practicality of Skinner's vision and the

need for revision in the original plan. Although sympathetic with the story of Twin Oaks, Skinner realized that there was still much to be done. In a foreword to Kathleen Kinkade's report, Skinner wrote: "Twin Oaks is simply the world in miniature. The problems it faces and the solutions it tries are those of a world community. While Kat and her friends seek solutions to their problems, the rest of the world must do something about *its* food supplies, *its* educational systems, *its* sanitation and health, *its* 'interpersonal' relations, *its* cultural activities, and *its* Olympic games."[3]

The almost tedious insistence on the application of behavioral science to "world affairs" is the result of the mature Skinner's belief in the high value of his work. The ultimate test of the worth of behaviorism will be behavioral rather than theoretical. The facts may or may not be pleasant and the philosophical implications for the future as well as the philosophical assumptions underwriting the original behaviorism may disturb or placate intellectuals but nothing *really* changes the issue: to survive or not to survive. The development of behavioral science during the three decades after *Walden Two* was notably in the direction of increased sophistication. As one studies Skinner's accomplishments, one notes some alterations in vocabulary and experimental designs, accompanied, however, by a constantly increasing confidence in his own rightness that makes him impatient with those who would exaggerate the significance of certain verbal concessions he has made over the years in the interests of better communication with a wider audience. The accessibility of his ideas to nonspecialists in *Walden Two* has perhaps overemphasized the importance of the work in Skinner's canon, and since it was written only seven years after *The Behavior of Organisms*, his first significant publication, it contains more youthful enthusiasm and less caution than later publications. Significantly, that enthusiasm has challenged fear and ignorance more effectively than his more sober reports of systematic experiments. Finally, however, the darkling plain of a dream-projection is not the most appropriate place to fight for Skinner's cause. The current issues transcend any man's dream of happiness. The battle of Walden Two is only one episode in the war between behavioral science and its enemies. *Can* there be—and even if there *can* be—*should* there be a rigorous science of human behavior? Only if human beings are allowed to be the proper stuff for science to study then may one hope that they are also the proper stuff that dreams of the Good Life are made on.

CHAPTER 3

The Highest Human Dignity

M OST people respect science and scientists as useful. They depend upon scientists to solve energy crises, cure diseases, and resolve economic depressions. They do not object to scientists' measuring things like water, earth, and air. They are amused when physicists, for example, correctly predict the behavior of teeter-totters and spaceships. When scientists, however, aspire to measure man himself they are accused of heresy, for the measure of man was destined to remain mysterious. In simple fact, man does initiate an infinite regress when he begins to measure himself measuring himself, and thus theoretically there will always be a residuum of the unmeasured. Scientists, however, believe that the residuum can be constantly decreased even if absolute knowledge must remain asymptotic to the goal of knowing everything about everything. Skinner, therefore, had not hesitated to propose a science of human behavior as the only way to increase knowledge about human behavior. In 1953 he wrote: "We may console ourselves with the reflection that science is, after all, a cumulative progress in knowledge which is due to man alone, and that the highest human dignity may be to accept the facts of human behavior regardless of their momentary implications."[1]

I Identify the Contingencies!

Although Skinner later proposed to take mankind not only beyond freedom but also beyond dignity, he did not abdicate his original commitment to knowing everything that could be known. For the old command "Know thyself," which was meant to stimulate intuitive self-knowledge, Skinner substituted a new command: "Identify the contingencies of reinforcement." This new command outraged defendants of the old faith. They protested without understanding and often as reflexively as Skinner could have predicted that Skinner was trying to decipher the ways of God Himself. They were not entirely wrong, for like Job before the voice in the whirlwind silenced him into awful submission, Skinner was seeking reasons for obvious afflictions, trying to understand the absurdities in creation itself. He was questioning the way of the world without indulging in the sweet self-pity of the world's martyrs. Job was finally overwhelmed with the simple logic of the whirlwind because in Job's day mere man had not yet put his own stars in the heavens, seeded the skies to produce rain, explored the moon, and defeated both the small and the great pox.

When Job was forced to concede that he could never uncover and thus never hope to understand the causes of his afflictions, to say nothing of the reasons for other absurdities in creation, he began to accept his suffering as inevitable. God won hands down, and Job achieved a rationalized peace by giving up his search for reasons. As he abdicated his right to know things, his afflictions disappeared. Thus he was reinforced for ceasing to ask questions. Job gave up trying to be sensible. He settled for magic and mystery.

Job was relatively lucky, however, for later Jobs have not always found such happy endings through ignorance and faith. Yet patience has usually been glorified as its own reward. Men have been conditioned to expect very little on this earth from the kind of Providence that seems to reinforce only erratically and intermittently those virtues recommended by moralists. Unlike Job, Skinner did not accept his ignorance as the better part of his humanity. He began early to check rhetoric against fact and to demand authoritative references from whirlwinds and scientists alike. Even the scientist is not the final authority, of course. The subject matter always knows best, Skinner has insisted over and over again. Be that as it may, Skinner saw no point in arguing about events that could be observed or in debating about events that could not be observed. In his lawful search for lawfulness he seemed to beg the question of the significance of lawfulness—just as all scientists do—but he minimized theory and the setting up of elaborate hypotheses to be checked against, and thus he could spend most of his time in the laboratory rather than at his desk.

Despite logical problems, if human behavior is most meaningful when it is not lawful, conceivably the behavioral scientist could establish once and for all the fact of whimsicality (maybe even

transcendent intentions) in his subjects' behavior. Sentimentalists
have made much of the physicist's reliance on indeterminacy—often by false analogy—yet without rigorous physical
science such apparently unpredictable events as misbehaving quan-
ta would not have been "discovered" despite the fact they really
have always been doing or not doing what they *really* have or have
not been doing without regard to debates about their actions. By
betting on law and order science is well situated to observe even a
so-called miracle dispassionately. A miracle, by definition, is an
event for which up to the time of its happening there was no
probability of its happening. Thus, if a given miracle occurs even
once, it moves over into the category of a real event. The miracle
becomes a fact and can be assigned a certain predictability.
Interestingly enough, some theologians insist on proof that the
alleged miracle has taken place, and in order to validate the event
call upon "scientific evidence" and also rate the "reliability" of the
witnesses. Careful scientists always assume a high probability that
alleged miracles are not divine sleight-of-hand performances to awe
the humble but rather glimpses into orderly processes as yet un-
charted.

II *A Manifesto:* Science and Human Behavior

A faith which is dependent upon accidents is first skeptical of
rationalism and ultimately cynical toward Providence. Scientists are
less cynical "believers" despite their professional skepticism.
Skinner's *Science and Human Behavior* (1953) is an early credo:
"Science is first of all a set of attitudes. It is a disposition to deal
with the facts," the staunch behaviorist asserted, "rather than with
what someone has said about them" (12). Although behavioral
science demands a strong commitment to those facts, it is not static,
for all facts in science are subject to alteration as the evidence alters.
Thus Skinner did not find it necessary to equate the indeterminacy
of quantum mechanics with humanistic unknowables. By 1953 he
had dismissed that phantom problem easily when he wrote the
following:

It has sometimes been pointed out . . . that physical science has been unable to maintain its philosophy of determinism, particularly at the sub-
atomic level. The Principle of Indeterminacy states that there are circumstances under which the physicist cannot put himself in possession of
all relevant information: if he chooses to observe one event, he must relin-

quish the possibility of observing another. In our present state of knowledge, certain events therefore appear to be unpredictable. It does not follow that these events are free or capricious. Since human behavior is enormously complex and the human organism is of limited dimensions, many acts may involve processes to which the Principle of Indeterminacy applies. It does not follow that human behavior is free, but only that it may be beyond the range of a predictive or controlling science. Most students of behavior, however, would be willing to settle for the degree of prediction and control achieved by the physical sciences in spite of this limitation. A final answer to the problem of lawfulness is to be sought, not in the limits of any hypothetical mechanism within the organism, but in our ability to demonstrate lawfulness in the behavior of the organism as a whole. (17)

Lawfulness is not merely assumed. If it were not demonstrable, the scientist would discard the assumption. Varying the agents outside the organism causes changes in the observable behavior of that organism. For example, a flash of light is followed by the contracting of the pupil of the organism's eye. There is also an obvious relationship between a sip of lemon juice and the flow of saliva, between the raising of the temperature outside the body and the behavior of blood vessels in the skin. These relationships are lawful but they are examples of simple reflexes, and although they do occur, Skinner has never claimed for them the major role in behavior. "We now see," he carefully explained, "that the principle of the reflex was overworked. The exhilarating discovery of the stimulus led to exaggerated claims. It is neither plausible nor expedient to conceive of the organism as a complicated jack-in-the-box with a long list of tricks, each of which may be evoked by pressing the proper button. The greater part of the behavior of the intact organism is not under this primitive sort of stimulus control" (49 - 50).

Those who oppose in principle a science of behavior often cite simple conditioning as Skinner's explanations for all human behavior, believing that Skinner had tried to reduce humans to noncognitive, reflexive organisms without inner causes. There is some subtle irony, however, in the situation. Although humans allegedly are not animals, household pets have often been elevated to humanoid status by sentimentalists who earnestly praise the lower creature's fidelity without seeming to realize that such fidelity is a dramatic example of noncognitive, reflexive responses, namely, Pavlovian conditioning to food and caresses. At the same time that pets are prized for not biting the hands that feed them, humans are urged to resist the kind of conditioning that short-circuits free choice. In fact, human love is supposedly debased if conditioned rather than freely given. Finally, it would seem that dogs are loved for those very qualities their owners despise in humans. Pets are prized for their thoughtless, automatic, and venal habits. No wonder early behavioral scientists experimented almost exclusively with rats and pigeons. Humans must have seemed much too confused until their rationalizations could be transformed into verbal behavior under identifiable controls.

III   Of Rats and Men

Pavlov's famous experiments with the dogs that learned to salivate at the ringing of bells, led to observations which were reportable in quantitative terms. Pavlov measured the time elapsing between the presentation of the stimuli and the responses. He also measured the responses by weighing the saliva produced. Pavlov's explanations, however, inevitably referred to hypothetical constructs, such as nonobservable cortical changes in his subjects. Such explanations were obviously fictitious. At best they could become hypotheses to be checked on, but whether they turned out to be true or false would be irrelevant to the status of Pavlov's measurements. These measurements were the data Skinner was interested in. Because only these "quantitative relations" could be observed, Skinner preferred to call *them* the facts rather than resort to hypothetical constructs inferring another event *inside* the organism. When he used the same approach in experimenting with human subjects, he was accused of overlooking human attributes such as man's will. Thus he was denounced for equating men with rats. The fact, however, that differences between a rat and a man become increasingly obvious as the same experimental techniques are used with both, was soon established. Comparative studies of the repertory of conditionable "operant" behavior in men and animals does not *per se* either strip the former of their humanity or anthropomorphize the latter. Resistance to extinction of any habit may still be man's finest characteristic, even if demonstrably conditionable and thus no longer to be called "freedom." Man's household pets, for example, are seldom encouraged to resist being housebroken or to refuse to obey, for man would find freedom in animals a nuisance. Humans, in effect, are conditioned to denounce only human conditioning. Otherwise they cheerfully train both their pets and children to obey.[2] Skinner, aware of the irony, insisted that only the observable relationships between behaving and the effect of that behavior are useful as explanations of the persistence or disappearance of that behavior. Other explanations may be pleasantly reinforcing but cannot be checked on, that is, cannot be handled *scientifically.*

The definitive account of operant conditioning includes technicalities intelligible only to specialists, although the cumulative knowledge has already reached that peculiar degree of sophistication in which the implications of behavioral science are more easily grasped—and thus more widely resented by nonspecialists—at the advanced level than at the elementary level. Something similar has happened in all science. Psychology has been slower, however, in clearing out the accumulation of untestable theories and wishful thinking so that students of psychology are often forced to learn various traditional fictions at the introductory stages of their study, only to be informed later, say in graduate school, that most cognitive and physiological psychology is not relevant to a *science* of human behavior. Just as the history of medicine is of only limited value to a physician, the history of how psychology broke away from philosophy and then later subsumed philosophy when American psychologists first expanded and then contracted their explanatory fictions, is of limited use to behavioral scientists today. Alchemy and conjuring are no longer required courses in medical schools despite the fact that verbal behavior still seems magical in its effects. If that behavior which Skinner was the first to define as operant conditioning plus those Pavlovian reflexes now called instrumental conditioning really describe all learned behavior, and if unlearned behavior is under the control of genetic factors already given in each organism, then nothing in any animal or human behavior is free of control. The fact that the identifying of controls is itself also not a free act is only a logical dilemma rather than a behavioral one. The only possible resolution to the putative impasse is for the scientist to proceed as if human behavior were completely determined while noting that he often "feels" that it is not. Eventually he will stop worrying about the apparent contradiction as new ways of accounting for that "feeling" emerge, particularly in the area of verbal behavior.

IV   *Cause and Effect*

Even casual observers of human behavior see a relationship between doing certain things and the effect of doing those things.

When the American psychologist Thorndike observed the behavior of cats, he parsimoniously explained certain aspects of cat behavior as the result of what the cats were doing. In the simplest experiment, the cat was placed in a kind of puzzle box from which it could escape only by unlatching a door. "Sensible" cats learned to unlatch the door and escape. Those who never learned how to escape presumably were removed by the experimenter before they died of confinement. In any event, the ultimate fate of the duller cats as well as the cruel experimenters remains moot, for no one is certain whether it is kinder to keep animals dumb or to educate them.

Such an apparently simple thing as escaping from a box, however, is not such a simple thing after all either for cats or for humans if one focuses on the means whereby the creature learns to escape rather than on the fact of escape. The escape itself is presumably reinforcing, for nonconfinement is rewarding when nonconfinement is associated with being fed and being patted after the organism has been deprived of food and love. Those who like to believe that both cats and humans "think" their way to freedom are only describing the events which lead to nonconfinement in pleasantly familiar but scientifically useless terms, for it is the behavior from which the thinking is inferred that is the relevant datum. Also, of course, it is the breaking out that finally counts, not just "thinking" about doing it.

Thorndike used the time it took each cat to get out of the box as his datum. His final data were collections of individual performances, averaged and plotted on a graph. This record came to be called a "learning curve." The smoothed-out shape of the curve, which was partly a function of averaging great numbers of cases so that errors and fumbles were nicely distributed on both sides of the average, was impressive. Learning seemed to be negatively accelerated: that is, the learner makes fast progress at first, then slows down his rate of progress as he nears the goal that Thorndike assigned to the learner. Cats in the Thorndike box were not rewarded for learning how *not* to escape from the box; by definition that was not the project. As a matter of fact, in some labs, certain rats, cats, and pigeons used to be arbitrarily dismissed and called "poor subjects" if they failed to give smooth curves as they pushed levers, unlatched doors, or pecked at targets. Recently more sophisticated experimenters have selected their subjects, animals and humans alike, with somewhat less ingenuous eagerness to get smooth curves, so that logically random samplings of organisms might today include some dead ones—subjects who give no curves at all.

Scientists also no longer necessarily believe everything humans say. Thorndike's cats, animals by definition and thus not having anything to say or unwilling or unable to say, were not questioned about anything and because they looked like cats the experimenters never asked them what they were. However, now that chimps are being trained to talk, some chimps may say they are humans and some humans may claim to be chimps, so it is still best not to believe any subject's verbal report about itself. Anyway, the subject is the last to know what it really is. That information is much less relevant than stubborn humanists (or resilient chimps who have learned to call themselves humanists) insist. Facetiousness aside, the conscientious psychologist who wants to be sure his subjects are humans has more and more trouble ascertaining that fact than laymen and even careless anthropologists suspect.

Scientifically it has always been safer to watch the subject's behavior than to question him and then believe his answers. The popularity of so-called lower animals as subjects for experimentation relates to the fact that talking confounds behavioral data unless, of course, the data are words, in which case the experimenter begins by recording the acoustical properties of the response rather than assuming stable, lexical meanings. The datum is always behavior to a behavioral scientist. Human subjects, when encouraged to give verbal reports about themselves, are conditioned to feel that they can help the experimenter by commenting. Such comments are properly part of behavior, but they are not necessarily any more informative than any other part. That is, human verbalizations are not always the most reliable indexes to what is going on either inside or outside the subject. The human capacity for *not* telling the truth, which is at once the most exciting characteristic of literature and the hallmark of courtesy and kindness, must not be overlooked in the laboratory, nor do simple instructions to tell the truth safeguard against lying, for the human being is no more capable of reporting fully and accurately than the nonspeaking animal.[3] It is the function of the scientist to observe all of the subject's behavior rather than simply converse with him. All verbalizations must be considered as objectively as any other aspect of behavior and used only with caution as meaningful utterances defined by the occasion of their utterance and the past history of the utterer.

Skinner has insisted that a science of human behavior can take into account all these marginal areas, including the failures of nerve and other situations which once seemed unpredictable. The Pavlovian conditioned reflex, which by-passes cortical functions associated traditionally with cognition, obviously does not adequately describe the genesis of that behavior which humanity is most interested in. If wars, for example, occur because people have been conditioned to associate shooting with glory, then fighting could be easily reconditioned by associating shooting with death—certainly a logical association. Presumably then there would be no more wars among people who want to live. But such simple reconditioning, Skinner discovered, seldom works. That people kill people in order not to be killed by people makes no sense. Ergo: although people are not sensible organisms, they are predictably nonsensible. Their silliness, in a word, is orderly. They are only *psychologically* understandable, never *logically*.

Making war is obviously a kind of behavior which persists for reasons other than the need to survive. War does change the environment, and if fighting is conditioned, something different from simplistic meat-and-bell association is happening. Salivating at a bell ringing is much like obeying orders to do something useless and ineffective, even wasteful; nevertheless, a small part of human behavior is certainly under such controls. The flash of light which "causes" the pupil of the eye to contract can be made to "cause" an ear to twitch through the process of association even though light is not an adequate or normal stimulus for ear twitching.

Such twitches are apparently on a kind of closed circuit, one which has been called the autonomic nervous system. The involuntariness is so obvious that twitchers who twitch in certain ways that the community by and large does not twitch in are said to be nervous or possessed of the devil. They are seldom accused of twitching *on purpose*. One's twitch is not one's own fault. Usually when the moralist decides that a bit of behavior is willfully bad, he assumes some other mechanism or some other circuit at work. Behavior for which no automatic circuit inside the body seems responsible is more dramatic and more controversial. Thus the will has become a convenient fiction with which to account for these functions. The will, however, explains nothing but itself in terms of itself, for allegedly man is able to will either to use his will or not to use his will so that there must be a will-of-wills and a will-of-the-will-of-wills, *ad infinitum*. Science cannot refer its causes to the fictitious will without sacrificing its objectivity. Nobody sane believes in the will of the rock to disintegrate or the will of the air to pollute itself. It is equally apparent to note that no sane man would will disasters.

How, then, do organisms, including humans, happen to do what they do? *How* shall the accountability for what is done be distributed? These questions are answerable, and, of course, are scientifically preferable to the meaningless *why* questions: *Why* did you do what you did? *Why* did you will to do wrong when you know it does not pay? Such *why* questions are best answered with a simple *because I did. How* questions demand an analysis of the occasion and the effect. The answers to *how* questions are useful to science.

V *Stamping In*

Thorndike called the process by which habits are learned "stamping in." Something continues to be done because there is a consequence which impresses the organism. In *Science and Human Behavior* Skinner describes the process from the point of view of the experimenter "working" with a pigeon:

We select a relatively simple bit of behavior which may be freely and rapidly repeated, and which is easily observed and recorded. If our experimental subject is a pigeon, for example, the behavior of raising the head above a given height is convenient. This may be observed by sighting across the pigeon's head at a scale pinned on the far wall of the box. We first study the height at which the head is normally held and select some line on the scale which is reached only infrequently. Keeping our eye on the scale we then begin to open the food tray very quickly whenever the head rises above the line. If the experiment is conducted according to specification, the result is invariable: we observe an immediate change in the frequency with which the head crosses the line. We also observe, and this is of some importance theoretically, that higher lines are now being crossed. We may advance almost immediately to a higher line in determining when food is to be presented. In a minute or two, the bird's posture has changed so that the top of the head seldom falls below the line which we first chose. (63 - 64)

The most important aspect of this neat experiment is the setting up of a contingency. Only when the pigeon behaves in a certain way does its behavior result in getting fed. In one sense the pigeon is learning moral behavior: it is learning that its behavior has consequences. There is, nevertheless, no need to infer that the pigeon has "thought" anything out or has "decided" to make wise choices. Obviously the pigeon can just as easily be encouraged to make silly choices. Explanations of its behavior do not require even such relatively austere fictions as "trial and error learning" or "the acquiring of habits" which are then filed away somewhere in its cortex. "The barest possible statement of the process," Skinner insisted, "is this: we make a given consequence contingent upon certain physical properties of behavior (the upward movement of the head), and the behavior is then observed to increase in frequency" (64).

An understanding of the pigeon's behavior includes the fact of the experimenter's control of the situation, namely, his ability to make a predicted increase in frequency "come true." This "barest possible statement of the process" is the only one, Skinner felt, that a scientist can settle for if he is true to his method. Any part of the description which does not relate to control and prediction and consequences is irrelevant. Moralists, of course, have also stressed the importance—but not the dominating prevalence—of consequences. The child is told again and again that his behavior produces certain effects. Often, however, the child does not understand until he touches the hot stove himself, drives while drunk, forgets to take precautions, smokes his first cigarette, or swallows his first drink. Each event is the first event of a chain of events which will follow it, and alcoholics can be "taught" that the consequence of taking one drink (even the heaviest drinkers drink no more than one drink at a time) changes the probability of taking subsequent drinks. Although no one can control a drink-already-taken, one feels some control over the drink-as-yet-untaken.

The fact that the future seems so real and thus seems to exert an effect on the present is largely a verbal artifact. Control refers itself to future events only insofar as the consequence of that control refers to future events. For young children, controls are at first quite contemporaneous and located outside the organism in the form of fences and babysitters. Teaching children not to get run over by a car could be done efficiently by letting them experience again and again the consequences of getting run over. Such efficiency, however, would be too efficient. It would cut down on accidents by eliminating children. Other devices for increasing the probability of desirable behavior, from moral maxims to spankings, are less efficient but obviously more humane. They must therefore be evaluated against long-term criteria.

All scientists are trained to observe before predicting or controlling. It was logical enough that behavioral scientists would begin by identifying the significant operants and then experiment with how to make those operants more likely or less likely to happen. The experiments consisted of manipulating the controlling reinforcements. Such "tampering" is moot mostly in name only, for few humans desire less than that things should work and that what they themselves do should count. Everyone wants to be effective. How neat it is, therefore, to discover that behavior which is effective is behavior which is rewarded. The beautiful simplicity of Skinner's operants has eluded many aestheticians only because they do not understand. Furthermore, in operant conditioning, just as any moralist might prescribe, *the organism must work for its rewards.*

VI *Measuring*

Although Skinner's measuring of human activities annoys both aestheticians and moralists, there can be no science without measuring. In all fairness, it is only the use to which any measuring is put that is problematic. The measure of Pavlovian conditioning, for example, is the magnitude of the response and the time it takes to get the response. Size and time are honorable measures of such simple events. Their usefulness is seldom challenged in nonhuman contexts. Most people know how much they weigh and how old they are, feeling such statistics, although quite personal, must be accepted as matters of fact.

Because in operant conditioning the reinforcement follows the response the organism is making, the most useful measure of such behavior is the rate of responding. From such a statistic the probability of the future behavior of the organism can be estimated. Anyway one slices it, with Ockham's razor or homemade machete, scientists are expected to make predictions about the future. Because the only data available come from the past history of the organism and its present activity, Skinner never quibbled about the subtle differences between probability theories. He used the simplest, perhaps the only valid one: a measure based upon past occurrences of an observable class of events. The only novelty in his approach was his emphasis on the rate of responding and his disregard of eliciting stimuli.

It is well to remember that even Newton could not be sure about the future behavior of all apples attached to stems attached to trees. After many observations he assumed that so many apples had fallen in the past that they would *most likely* continue to fall in the future rather than soar upward. That the sun will rise tomorrow morning is a probability based on the observation of past sunrises and not a guarantee about tomorrow's dawn. Yet most people easily settle for high probabilities as certainties. Although statisticians have worked out critical ratios for reasonable credibility, Skinner opted for the least elaborate of tests of significance: the patterns of a subject's behavior over extended periods of time.

Skinner emphasized the fact that operant conditioning "shapes behavior as a sculptor shapes a lump of clay." The behavior is not simply elicited by a bit of energy in the environment but grows, as it were, in the hands of the sculptor, who here, of course, symbolizes the environment. The metaphor is apt and Skinner made the most of it in *Science and Human Behavior:* "Although at some point the sculptor seems to have produced an entirely novel object, we can always follow the process back to the original undifferentiated lump, and we can make the successive stages by which we return to this condition as small as we wish. At no point does anything emerge which is very different from what preceded it. The final product seems to have a special unity or integrity of design, but we cannot find a point at which this suddenly appears. In the same sense, an operant is not something which appears full grown in the behavior of the organism. It is the result of a continuous shaping process" (91).

The sculptor-clay metaphor is not in itself an objectionable one. Pious people have been addressing the Creator in the same terms for ages: "Have Thy own way, Lord, have Thy own way: Thou art the potter, I am the clay." Human beings are generally said to be fashioned by *something.* The environment has always been credited with a major role, but it was itself traditionally considered an attribute of the Creator who *intended* it to serve as a polishing agent. Just how predetermined or purposive the aggregates of causes and effects in environmental conditioning may be is a teleological problem. In behavioral science the problem is resolved by defining goals as post-facto events. *Anything* that the organism is likely to approach as the result of having been reinforced on previous approaches is defined as a goal. The future does not exist. As a mere probability projection from the past the future appears to motivate today's behavior, but the real future always remains in the future and thus is never real. Anxiety about the future, which is a present event, does count, of course, insofar as a fictitious future has become presently threatening.

Skinnerians have experimented with elaborately varied schedules of reinforcement. Reinforcement can be made to occur as a function of time, as a function of number of response units, and as combinations thereof. Much behavior is reinforced only intermittently.

Skinner observed that everyday life is full of such patterns: "We do not always win at cards or dice, because the contingencies are so remotely determined that we call them 'chance.' We do not always find good ice or snow when we go skating or skiing. Contingencies which require the participation of people are especially likely to be uncertain. We do not always get a good meal in a particular restaurant because cooks are not always predictable. We do not always get an answer when we telephone a friend because the friend is not always at home. We do not always get a pen by reaching into our pocket because we have not always put it there. The reinforcements characteristic of industry and education are almost always intermittent because it is not feasible to control behavior by reinforcing every response" (99).

Behavioral science, literally determined to find lawfulness in all human actions, begins by redefining "will" and "choice" as "predisposition" and "probability." There is nothing necessarily vicious about trying to discover the effects of various schedules of reinforcement on behavior. The discovery, which began as a series of casual observations subsequently experimentally verified, that intermittent patterns of reinforcement are effective in sustaining habits and in setting up predispositions to resist extinction of these habits, was not Skinner's *fault*. He did not set out to dehumanize people. If *facts* are themselves dehumanizing, who dares to assert *that* as a fact? Here is the area in which the behavioral scientist admits complexities exist. His admission, however, is not a capitulation to a bad conscience, for a pure behaviorist feels uncomfortable—possibly suffers conscience-pains—when he does not know the facts. The removal of that uncomfortableness is reinforcing. To use ordinary terms, in the presence of ignorance he feels something akin to a saint's anxiety in the face of evil. Like a saint, he seeks relief in action. Although theologians disagree about the role of good works in achieving salvation, scientists agree on the value of knowledge. Saints may lose the reward of martyrdom by pursuing it too determinedly but scientists are "in error" unless hot after certainty. They demand answers to their *how* questions at all costs. Also, they are more interested in the effects of variations than in establishing a transcendent unity.

VII   *Reinforcement Schedules*

"It is important," Skinner noted, "to distinguish between schedules which are arranged by a system outside the organism and those which are controlled by the behavior of the organism itself. An example of the first is a schedule of reinforcement which is determined by a clock—as when we reinforce a pigeon every five minutes, allowing all intervening responses to go unreinforced. An example of the second is a schedule in which a response is reinforced after a certain number of responses have been emitted—as when we reinforce every fiftieth response the pigeon makes. The cases are similar in the sense that we reinforce intermittently in both, but subtle differences in the contingencies lead to very different results, often of great practical significance" (100).

When behavior is reinforced steadily at fixed intervals of time, the rate of responding is affected. The subject begins to slow down immediately after each reinforcement, appearing to "realize" that a certain time must pass before another reward is forthcoming, appearing to "decide" that he might just as well wait until it pays to go back to work. So-called variable-interval reinforcement, however, steadies the rate of response. When the intervals at the end of which reinforcement occurs are varied so that sometimes the interval is stretched to six or seven minutes and at other times it is shortened to two or three minutes, the behavior of the subject is stabilized. The organism appears to "learn" that it might as well keep responding at a steady rate no matter how erratic the rewarding schedule, for in such a situation rewards are predictable only on the average. As an analogy, Skinner describes how a salesman learns to persist in trying to sell even during long stretches of time in which he sells nothing. His objective is to sell over a long period the average of his quota. The real-estate broker who never sells anything may persist in trying to sell only if there are reinforcements other than commissions. Thus one can reasonably conclude that so-called heroism, which is behavior in the face of almost certain defeat, is conditionable. It is thus possible to engineer aggressive and militant behavior in apparently hopeless situations. In fact, the more hopeless, the more resistant to extinction a defense can become as a function of intermittent, aperiodic reinforcements cleverly encouraging so-called loyalty, for example, to a lost cause.

The kind of intermittent reinforcement which manipulates *numbers* of responses is even more dramatic in its effect on behavior. When a pigeon is reinforced after every fiftieth pecking, it learns to work hard and fast for food; that is, this particular reinforcement schedule generates a high rate of response. In industry, workers are often paid after every fifty units of production such as after fifty pieces of finished goods. This ratio-reinforcement schedule, Skinner observed, is common in education. Students are usually reinforced for completing a defined project such as a term paper. In the same way wars may never be won, but molehills can be defended if enough medals are forthcoming after each skirmish—successful or not.

Experimental situations are designed, of course, to establish the limits of effectiveness of any of these schedules of reinforcement. Fatigue, which is detected by the failure of the organism to respond, follows overextending the period in which no reinforcement is forthcoming. To account for discouragement or inaction as the result of overextending the number of units of work required without forthcoming rewards seems at first too obvious to be significant; however, when reinforcement schedules for human beings are designed to minimize such fatigue, trouble begins. Describing fatigue as "lack of will" while also explaining fatigue as *caused* by a "lack of will" makes little sense. It is not necessarily a person's fault if he gets tired. All one needs to know is the conditions which lead to tiredness in order to minimize one's tiredness in the future. Unfortunately the descriptive term "fatigue" often encourages emotional responses which lead to useless exhortations to "snap out of it." Athletes have learned how effective chemical stimulants are in temporarily overcoming the feeling of fatigue. Interestingly enough, athletes are openly encouraged to get more sleep while they are covertly being supplied with more stimulants. Sportsmen at first encourage natural conditions in their horses and quarterbacks but if their favorites are not winners, they are willing to accelerate those natural conditions by rewarding the subjects for working more and more strenuously to reach the arbitrary goal. Such reinforcement schedules emerge as a product of the competition and obviously encourage cheating. Thus Skinner would discourage such escalating competition in an ideal community. In any event, conditioning is part of all life, although there is a more important kind of conditioning than was dreamed of in Pavlov's laboratory. While Pavlov seemed to urge his dogs to try harder and harder just as a fan cheers his team to victory, Skinner unsettled many clichés about the will to win.

In Pavlovian conditioning the controlling stimuli, such as the odor of the meat and the sound of the bell, were so easy to identify that no one could deny their relationship to the dog's changing behavior. The salivating of the conditioned dog at the sound of the bell after meat and bell had been associated was clearly "caused" by that association. The stupendous possibility that all learning was simply such conditioning had occurred to early behaviorists, but Skinner saw almost at once that such a model would neither fit the most important kinds of human learning nor account for so-called intentional acts. At the same time he refused to rely on traditional fictions to explain those behavior patterns which remained inexplicable in terms of Pavlovian conditioning. He took a second look at behavior.

VIII   *The Heresy: Operant Conditioning*

Second looks promote heresy. Skinner's second looks discovered operant behavior. In behavior which has been operantly conditioned the responses are "emitted" rather than "elicited." Operant behavior is a function of the occasion. To change the response in Pavlovian conditioning, the experimenter simply changes the eliciting stimulus. In operant behavior, however, the whole situation is involved. For example, in a typical sports contest the cheers and music set the occasion for other behavior, such as buying tickets, shouting, exulting in victory or grieving in defeat. To Skinner the sports fan behaves somewhat like a poet. He is a nonsensible organism in that he demands victory at all times and shouts and stamps and even weeps to make his side exert itself, while all the time he must be aware that the other side is doing the same thing and that both sides cannot win despite their similar techniques. Something else must be the crucial factor. Wishing does not make it so, popular songs to the contrary. The fan is a poet who refuses to run critical experiments or to pay attention to evidence.

Pigeons, like fans, can also be conditioned to do strange things. Skinner discovered that healthy pigeons can learn ritualistic habits as well as survival habits. Pigeons can be trained to stretch their necks a certain distance whenever a light is shining in the experimental box by reinforcing the neck-stretching only when the light is on. When the light is off, no neck-stretching is reinforced so that particular ritual is extinguished by darkness and stimulated by light. The pigeon has learned to discriminate between the two situations. It is unnecessary to posit a will in a trained pigeon even though its ability to make discriminations often looks as if it was making decisions.

Such discriminative stimuli as light and darkness "share control" with other stimuli, but they were at first easily overlooked, particularly since there was such a strong predisposition (itself under the control of discriminative stimuli) to overlook them. As long as these stimuli were overlooked, "drives" and "motives" in pigeons as well as people were invented as causes. However, Skinner demonstrated that putative voluntary behavior, at least in pigeons, was really controlled by identifiable aspects of the environment. By extrapolation, the idea that people work at will to reach future goals began to be suspect.

Skinner's early extrapolations from pigeon-behavior to human behavior were bold but not unwarranted. He noticed that the kind of behavior in pigeons which was established accidentally as the result of a casual connection between a response and the appearance of an unexpected reinforcer resembles superstitious behavior in humans. Pigeons, however, Skinner concluded, were not really more gullible than people. When either a human or a pigeon is doing something at the moment something else occurs, that second something is associated with the first activity and thus can become reinforcing—*accidentally* so. The finding of a ten dollar bill, for example, strengthens the tendency to repeat whatever one was doing at the time of the accidental find, particularly whenever one is under money-deprivation.

Many verbal formulas are repeated again and again by superstitious people with only a minimal effect, or none at all if one discounts chance. Such formulas have become part of the culture and the saying of them is seldom checked on. In such behavior the ordinary processes of conditioning have occurred under special circumstances. The learning is essentially nonadvantageous but nevertheless persistent.

Such habits are not necessarily unimpressive just because they are demonstrably ineffective with reference to their *original* uses. Bad things happen every day, and enough bad things happen on Friday the thirteenth to "prove" that Friday the thirteenth is an unlucky day if the predisposition to believe is there. The knowledge that children first acquire about alleged bad-luck days is usually secondhand. They learn to *say* that Friday-the-thirteenth is unlucky, and for merely *saying* so they get rewarded. In contrast, nonsuperstitious people more frequently check their behavior, particularly their verbalizations, against experience. They tend to keep that which works and to discard that which does not. Even William James, whose own pragmatism could not cure his insomnia, once employed the help of a Christian Science practitioner. After twelve "treatments" he testified that he could sleep better. Although he finally rejected the spiritual claims of Christian Science, he accepted the effects of the treatment. Charms and medals may not ward off the evil they were originally designed to thwart; yet displaying one of them may help one get accepted by a community in which they are highly valued.

IX   *Discriminative Repertoires*

Skinner eagerly investigated and clarified the organism's "discriminative repertoires," that is, those bits of behavior under the control of certain secondary stimuli. He concluded early in his studies that "attention," for example, which is traditionally defined as voluntary control of the stimulus by the stimulated, is not voluntary at all. It is instead behavior in which an individual is trained to attend to one situation rather than to possible alternatives. One acquires a repertoire of such "choices" over a period of time. Reading is usually a reinforcing activity; thus the reading of billboards along a highway takes precedence over looking at scenery not because one chooses to neglect the road but because one *can do nothing else!* One looks not because he wills to do so but because he has been rewarded for looking in the past. The expression "taking an interest in," Skinner decided, was only an awkward way of describing the consequences of operant conditioning. If, of course, the reading driver crashes, he may "learn" new consequences of reading, namely, that reading while driving is not as positively reinforcing as reading alone has been.

Inevitably Skinner rejected the definition of "ability" as something a person freely utilizes or equally freely rejects. It seemed to him that the time spent scolding students for having ability which they do not use is time wasted just as it would be foolish to exhort pigeons to work harder. Time is better spent in stimulating the student to do whatever the so-called latent ability was supposed to make it possible for him to do if he had so willed. Also, Skinner argued, without a person's *doing* something there was no way of checking on his *knowing* something. One does if he can, does not if he cannot. *Willing* an act is a fiction. If one can, one will or will not do what one can as a function of relevant variables—most of them outside the actor. There are sets of circumstances under which a person does or does not behave appropriately. The appropriateness, of course, is judged so or not so by the members of the community, or by inanimate forces which destroy the actor if he behaves inappropriately. Thus the observed frequency of what one was doing in the past under certain circumstances seemed to Skinner the most useful measure of any ability to perform similarly either now or in the future. Importantly, capacity is never properly inferred from anything other than past behavior.

Because the world is real its properties exist and are explorable. Those properties, however, are not simply there or not there. They exist along gradients of strength. In the same way an organism possesses varying thresholds of sensitivity. Although the relationships between stimuli and responses are often subtle, presumably the lawfulness of those relationships can ultimately be established. That established lawfulness is the scientist's "knowing," to achieve which he designs experiments and observes behavior under controlled conditions. For example, he notes that when pecking responses of a pigeon to a circular red spot are reinforced while responses to circular spots of other colors are not reinforced, the pigeon eventually pecks at circular red spots only but not to all redness or all roundness. The pigeon has learned to discriminate rather than to abstract. To achieve abstracting behavior, responses to variously shaped red objects are reinforced, so that the organism learns to respond to redness of any size or shape. The purity of the abstraction, however, is always threatened by other previously reinforced qualities of the stimulus, for the past experience of the organism has already "influenced" it. In humans, the name for that particular aspect of an object or event being responded to becomes important. Thus certain philosophers have supposed that the whole process is linguistic. The fact is, however, that the "subtle properties of nature" which abstracting responds to are observable only as those responses; that is, they are properties only of behavior. If the response has *no* effect insofar as it is not followed by something which rewards the behaving organism, the response will disappear.

If Skinner has pointed man to the "nadir of ignominy" by searching out the lawfulness in human behavior, the most dramatic example is his exploration of man's language habits which traditionally have been supposed to be controlled by will or inspiration or at least related to deep structures and unconscious processes. If poets and prophets always speak predictably as conditioned organisms, Truth becomes a common noun and Epiphanies fall to existence. Skinner was not concerned, however, about either grammar or theology. The fact that men *work* for food, clothing, and money while they *talk* about faith, hope, and charity can be accounted for by Skinner. The poet, the preacher, and the merchant all reach for their visions as functions of similar variables. The sportsman, the con man, and the honest salesman all exploit the same principles. And mostly they all talk—use language.

Man's ability to talk, read, and write was formerly considered beyond the ken of mere psychologists, so it had been entrusted to philosophers, many of whom specialized in languages and became linguists. Yet Skinner was not convinced that the principal difference between rats and men had ever been accurately measured much less approached as behavior available to observation, prediction, and control. Because language is so important, Skinner's investigation of language as verbal behavior has been the most controversial part of his program. To defend Skinner as the first scientific linguist arouses watch dogs who bark *meaningfully*. It is a delicate operation but nonetheless must be undertaken, for it is at the heart of the whole matter.

CHAPTER 4

Man in the Box

E ARLY in his career Skinner hazarded a prediction "that the only differences I expect to see revealed between the behavior of rat and man (aside from enormous differences of complexity) lie in the field of verbal behavior."[1] Inevitably Skinner was accused of reducing the articulating human being to a talking rat and of trying to put complex men into simplistic training boxes. What Skinner intended to announce, however, was an extension of the rigorous methodology of his earlier work on animals to the study of man's highest glory—his language habits. Man in the Skinner box need be neither mute nor unimaginative.

A science of human behavior that delegates the control of man's speaking, writing and reading skills to ineffable and thus never-to-be identified inner forces would not be a science. Although Skinner did not ever, like John Watson, try to reduce all thinking to subvocal muscle responses, he has rigorously viewed all uses of language as behavior and thus as observable, controllable, and predictable. Refusing to hypothesize something mysterious inside the organism as the cause of the organism's verbal behavior, Skinner rejected a fictitious "mind" as a repository of "ideas," and, of course, "thinking" as the exclusive function of that so-called mind. All of these rejections, however, were strategic rather than the result of a stubborn unawareness of the fact that people honestly believe that their awareness is real and their decisions are autonomous.

I Man: A Talking Rat

Skinner's approach to the verbal behavior of humans is properly viewed as an extension of his approach to the nonverbal behavior of rats and pigeons, with due concern for the enormous increase in complexity. Rejecting "meaning" as inherent in letters or words, Skinner found nothing relevant in purely logical analyses of propositions and syllogisms. Not surprisingly, Skinner's explanations of how language works are referred to the laws of operant conditioning and thus are confusing or unintelligible to anyone who does not understand operant conditioning. Furthermore, all verbalizings to Skinner are data to be analyzed and manipulated according to the tried methods of science rather than purposive utterances to be analyzed rhetorically. The fact that Skinner's analyses and manipulations are always coolly specified so that any enthusiasm or despair at confronting those specifications is a response of the confronter and not of the experimenter has given Skinner the reputation of being indifferent if not hostile to literature and other "higher" uses of language. Skinner's most radical contentions, however, have always been explicitly scientific rather than polemical. He meant no offense to others, beyond identifying them as nonscientific, when he rejected all previous theorizings about speaking, writing, and reading as irrelevant to his study. Traditional and nontraditional linguists, it seemed to Skinner, had begged the critical questions by assuming either that words had innate meanings or that humans inherited the capacity to "understand" and use language with only a minimum of training. "Meaning" was meaningless for Skinner, however, and true to his science he first looked for external causes. As far as possible he emptied the human organism of intention and meaning. For a behaviorist the determinants of each language act fix its significance. Not surprisingly, Skinner was misunderstood when he wrote: "We observe that a speaker possesses a *verbal repertoire* in the sense that responses of various forms appear in his behavior from time to time in relation to identifiable conditions" (21). This "verbal repertoire" differs from the traditional vocabulary in that the latter refers to a storehouse of words presumably memorized (or inherited!) rather than "functional units" demonstrably under the control of identifiable factors. The storehouse concept implies that words wait in the memory of the speaker, writer, or listener until they are called up to match the caller's thoughts and observations. The building of vocabularies by increasing the number of words in the storehouse has generally been considered desirable, witness the missionary zeal of the promoters of dictionaries.

For most teachers, "Get the dictionary habit" has become a moral axiom. Although Skinner accepted dictionaries as repositories of conventional verbal associations—which, as such, can be useful—he carefully differentiated between behavioral significance and lexical definitions. That differentiation in itself was not completely new. Descriptive linguists had already insisted upon editing old dictionaries by adding new meanings. Skinner, however, took a more unequivocally radical position. Characteristically, Skinner refused to postulate an autonomous or intentional process in humans involving the calling forth of words by a person to match the ideas of that person. If he had done so, he would have been forced to account for the "ideas"—a level further removed from accessibility—as well as the internal automaton.

II *Intraverbal Responses*

In Skinnerian terms, a verbal unit is not necessarily a single word.[2] It is instead an operant which differs from nonverbal operants only so far as much verbal behavior is under the control of other verbal behavior and is remarkably independent of the amount of energy involved. This fact at first obscures the kinship of talking, writing, and reading to other learned behavior, such as dancing. Furthermore, Skinner distinguished three kinds of verbal operants in which the stimulus is itself verbal and for convenience named them "echoic, textual, and intraverbal." In echoic behavior the *sound* of one person's verbalization sets the occasion for another person's matching sound. In textual responses the shape of a visual hieroglyph, printed or written, sets the occasion for the response which is known as reading. In intraverbal behavior certain units set the occasion for "fill-in" responses of other units. In each of these three verbal operants the sound, the text, or a learned convention acts as a discriminative stimulus in the presence of which certain responses are presumably reinforcing to the behaving organism. The removal of aversive effects can also, it is well to remember, act as positive reinforcement. Many other subtleties also contribute to the contingencies which make verbal behavior "likely" to occur.

When a behavioral scientist says that a person has the ability to read, he means that there is information available about the probability that the same person will read *again* under certain conditions. The person has been observed to do so in the past and thus *may* do so again, depending upon the frequency of past performances by that person. Even nonscientists call upon their dogs to *perform* their tricks as proof that they can. It is not possible to take any dog's word for its repertoire of skills, of course, because dogs do not verbalize and thus must act out all skills rather than brag about them. It is easier to test animals because they are unable to utter lies. In fact it is meaningless to conclude that a pigeon "knows" its way home. More accurately, one records the frequency of former successful homeward flights of a given pigeon and then makes an educated guess about that pigeon's future flying. Similarly, it cannot sensibly be said of a human being that he knows a given language system until he has been observed *doing* the language effectively, that is, reading, writing, and speaking in a way that the language community responds to and thus reinforces. Certainly no child spontaneously speaks, reads, or writes any language to which he has not been exposed. The child may inherit the *capacity* to learn any language used by human beings, but he does not inherit a given language.

Intraverbal responses account for much of the familiar shape of a language. They are patterns and associations which a given community reinforces. Social formulas, Skinner noted, utilize this kind of verbal behavior. Small talk, for example, is generally "safe" because it consists of expected comments which are responses to other expected comments. Truth seldom intrudes when polite conversation dwindles to the exchange of stock phrases. A question such as "How are you?" more often than not sets the occasion for a predictable and thus noninformative response such as "Fine" even when the responding organism is sick. To discover how a friend *really* feels one usually repeats the question, adding "really." Better yet, one might also give the subject of one's concern a physical examination as well as a lie detector test and then compare his present performances with his past performances as well as the performances of others.

Most grammatical structures are also not very informative, for they are conventionalized and thus are predictable for an "educated" person. They are usually merely intraverbal chains rather than spontaneous responses to outside reality or to the needs of the organism. Consequently they provide little information about the speaker's "true" condition other than that he is literate or illiterate—that he has been conditioned by a certain kind of environment to which he was alert enough to respond. Although Skinner observes that certain words tend to occur together, to suppose this tendency is profoundly significant, as in word-association tests, is pretentious. Conventional intraverbal operants become a part of the repertoire of everyone exposed to a given language system. When they are spoken or written, these "emissions" reassure the auditor or reader that the situation is a familiar one and that it is safe for him to respond in kind.

Contrary to uninformed opinion, Skinner's analysis of language behavior is not completely skeptical of traditional meanings insofar as some verbalizing does relate to a reality that can be observed and agreed on. Many linguists are less alarmed by Skinner's treatment of so-called nonintraverbal responses, which he subdivides into three groups: the "mand," the "tact," and the "audience controlled response." These classes are defined by the external or internal environment, that is, by what sets the occasion for the behavior and by the reinforcers which follow that behavior.

III   *The Mand*

The kind of language response which involves a minimum number of variables Skinner named a "mand," deriving the term from both "command" and "demand" to indicate that it always asks something of reality. The mand is not identified by its formal characteristics but rather by controlling variables, by what makes it happen. It may look like a traditional verb or noun, but it is not necessarily either one. It is this emphasis on the defining characteristics as behavioral rather than formal which distinguishes the mand from intraverbal responses. Skinner resolved the favorite ambiguities of traditional linguists, who long ago also discovered that the form of a word does not always signal an unequivocal meaning, by simply rejecting the formal aspect of the ambiguity. For example, even words like "man" and "take," often identified by school children as noun and verb respectively, are easily converted into verb and noun respectively in the sentences "*Man* the oars" and "The *take* was considerable."

Examples of the true mand are available in the language only as behavior. Printed or written transcriptions are accurately perceived only as records of mands rather than as true mands. Although, as has been noted, mands may look like verbs or nouns to grammarians, looks alone are of no significance to a behaviorist. A living man is necessarily present when a true mand occurs. That live organism specifies the reinforcement. When a hungry man calls out "bread" or "soup," he is specifying the "ultimate reinforcement" of his mand. In some cases the speaker is asking for that which will satisfy him—and nothing else. In other cases, however, the speaker may also specify the behavior of the listener, as when he says, "Pass the salt!" Here he is asking for the thing (demanding) as well as for action (commanding) on the part of the listener. In order to account for the effectiveness of mands, an effectiveness that gives them much power, the "total speech episode" must be considered. Mands operate for the benefit of the speeaker, who eventually gets or does not get what he is manding. Since repeated mands can move an annoyed or bored listener to refuse to provide the state of affairs being manded, they are often subtly varied, as in flattery. Phrases like "please" and "thank you" are conventionally added to mands and then persist as speech habits to the extent that they are effective. Poets, however, use mands in a special way.

Although it has generally not been acknowledged by hostile critics, Skinner has honored rather than debased the event known as "making a poem." True, he has referred to the event as similar to producing a baby. For him poets emit poems—that is, have poems just as mothers have children. He has, however, properly identified the language of literature as different from that of science. While ideally the latter is sharply denotative, the former is obviously connotative, reflective, allusive, and metaphorical. What Skinner calls the "extended mand" subsumes such loose verbal behavior and properly describes the making of literature as well as the generating of so-called nonsense. Talking to dolls, for example, seldom results in any response from the doll, yet children do persist in such behavior. In talking nonsense the emitter of the mand apparently assumes that the listener or reader is unable to respond to the request, and thus the absence of response to the comment does not extinguish the behavior. Yet the case must be included as an example of operant behavior or Skinner has not accounted for all verbalizing. The reinforcement is there somewhere, of course—either in the behavior of responding organisms, such as parents and other children, or in the child itself. Such behavior is acceptable in children and poets. Usually, however, it is weakened (not reinforced) in the adult by the community's insistence on what it calls rational language, that is, verbal behavior in which the requests, demands, or commands could *really* be granted or obeyed. Furthermore, originally unreasonable manding, such as asking for the moon, can become reasonable as technology provides the means of granting the request, with the result that a poem can eventually seem quite prosaic. A request for a trip to the moon is no longer an imaginative mand but an attainable demand. A request to reverse time, however, is still considered hopelessly poetic. Manding a return to youth illustrates the speaker's or writer's resistance to the extinction of verbal habits which do not measurably change the universe in which he lives. Theologians may be disturbed by the possibility that it is precisely because prayers are unreasonable demands upon an unanswering universe and therefore not testable, that praying persists. The situation, however, is not unusual to a behaviorist.

"The speaker," according to Skinner, "appears to create new mands on the analogy of old ones. Having effectively manded bread and butter, he goes on to mand the jam, even though he has never obtained jam before in this way. . . . Flushed with our success under favorable reinforcing circumstances, we set out to change the world without benefit of listener. Unable to imagine how the universe could have been created out of nothing, we conjecture that it was done with a verbal response. It was only necessary to say, with sufficient authority, *Let there be light!*" (48). Surprisingly sensitive to literary values, Skinner cites many other examples of what he named "magical mands." Looking through anthologies he discovered that lyrical poetry was especially full of such evocations. "Go and catch a falling star," for example, is not the sort of command that anyone could ever obey, yet the verbal behavior persists because it has been generally reinforced, unit for unit, in other contexts.

IV *Audience Control and Tacting*

Two other classes of verbal responses are largely controlled by persons and things in the environment: verbal behavior which consists of responses to an audience of one or more persons, and verbal behavior which consists of naming perceivable aspects of reality, such as objects. In the first class, labeled by Skinner "audience control," a listener or putative reader exerts powerful control over the actor's behavior, which, of course, often includes activities other than verbal ones. Rituals, gestures, and the wearing of appropriate clothes occur or do not occur as the result of the presence or absence of other people. The nature of the audience encourages certain responses and discourages others. Just as a dog learns to drool in the presence of the master who feeds him because the presence of the master signals the occasion for feeding as well as the promise of food, so the presence of an audience sets the occasion for actions—and particularly for verbalizing—which is likely to be accepted and responded to positively by that audience. Of course the audience is seldom the *only* variable in the situation, and thus Skinner constantly stresses the fact that most verbalizing is multiply controlled.

Naming aspects of reality is also obviously important behavior. Largely under the control of things and situations, this class of verbal responses was named by Skinner the "tact," a term suggesting both contact with reality and diplomacy. The human capacity to give names to nonexistent objects and relationships is also a kind of "tacting," one which may be informally qualified as "sloppy tacting." Just as poets, for example, do not "mand" reasonably, they often "tact" inaccurately; yet poetic verbalizations are undeniably evocative if often meaningfully ambiguous. Skinner's systematic approach to language as behavior admits almost enthusiastically the existence as well as the importance of sloppy tacting and magical manding. Literature need not fear behaviorism.

To Skinner meaning is always relationship and never inherent in words, and thus his interest focused on *how* people behave verbally. The fact that Skinner's approach to language neither debases nor glorifies communication as such, is not always understood. For example, a speaker who is looking at one object as he emits a "word" while the listener is looking at a different object, one which the listener supposes the former is naming, inevitably miscommunicates. God may be present in the dancing daffodil, as a poet has implied, but if the reader, while testing the truth of the poem, looks at a canker worm in the blossom instead of at the glorious yellow petals, the poet's use of "flower" as a metaphorical tact for "God" miscommunicates badly. Yet it is important to know that man's capacity to make such mistakes, which are merely extensions of careful tacting, accounts for metaphors and similes. Interesting and even outrageous mistakes in meaning are not only predictable in poems but essential to all literature.

The scientist, in contrast, is encouraged to tact as precisely as possible. Although the poet tacts imaginatively, that is, as imprecisely as possible without sacrificing all chance reinforcement, he is also responding to his kind of reality and he is behaving lawfully. His words are observable, classifiable, and predictable. Somehow this fact disturbs poets more than it does scientists, although obviously most verbal behavior consists of illogical statements, clichés, redundancies, tautologies, and mere grunts. This fact did not disturb Skinner, however, for he was intent on observing *all* verbal behavior rather than passing judgments or prescribing rules.

Skinner once tested Shakespeare's diction for alleged poetic qualities and found that the famous sonnets do not contain any more alliteration than might be expected by chance.[3] He also demonstrated that some of the writing of Gertrude Stein was the predictable consequence of her experiments in automatic writing.[4] These facts do not in any way alter the possible aesthetic or philosophical value of the words of either Shakespeare or Stein. Perhaps poets are less mad than critics had feared and psychiatrists had assumed.

V *Noam Chomsky's Famous Review*

Those who respond negatively to Skinner's analysis of language and literature include both naive and informed persons. The absence of intentionality in operant behavior seemed less serious when pigeons were being trained than when potential poets were being "educated." Skinner's insistence on locating ideas in verbal articulations and then on describing that articulation as conditioned behavior variously frightened, disgusted, annoyed, and amused both professional linguists and amateur lingophiles, themselves conditioned, of course, to defend intentional cognition as cause rather than effect. In a now-famous review of Skinner's 1957 *Verbal Behavior*, Noam Chomsky, a distinguished lingust, allegedly disposed of Skinner's behavioral analysis of language for all time.[5] Chomsky's essay went virtually unanswered, not because it was unanswerable or invulnerable but because Skinner himself decided, after a look at the review, that Chomsky simply did not understand what Skinner was doing. It was intelligently answered after more than a decade by Kenneth MacCorquodale, who observed that the Chomsky review seemed "ungenerous to a fault" as well as "condescending, unforgiving, obtuse, and ill-mannered."[6] The reluctance of Skinner's followers to challenge Chomsky was probably motivated less by fear of their inability to refute him than it was by disgust at the triviality of the issue.

Finally in 1970, MacCorquodale wrote a seventeen-page rejoinder to Chomsky's attack on Skinner, in which he analyzed Chomsky's alleged refutations, identified those confrontations which are paradigmatic or epistemological; and to the satisfaction of Skinnerians, at least, discredited Chomsky's demolition of *verbal*

behaviorism. MacCorquodale's answer, however, did not im-
mobilize Chomsky, who has continued to voice his objections to
Skinnerism.[7] In general, Chomsky credits heredity more than
Skinner does with the essential "causes" of language behavior.
Chomsky emphasizes man's ability to utilize his "understanding" of
a language as a kind of *Gestalt,* thus making it unnecessary to account for all learning as the result of exposure to experience and
reinforcement. The tiresome debate over heredity versus environment should, however, finally be resolvable through experimentation.

MacCorquodale's analysis of the serious issues in the debate
recognizes that Skinner and Chomsky speak different languages.
His summing up of Chomsky's review is mildly provocative but also
reflects Skinner's personal detachment at the time from polemical
fun-and-games. Since this study concentrates on Skinner, MacCorquodale is here given the emphatic position. He concluded thus:

[Chomsky's] review completely ignored much that is central to an understanding, application and assessment of Skinner's position. Most importantly it failed to reflect Skinner's repeated insistence that the full adequacy
of his explanatory apparatus for complex cases, including verbal behavior,
cannot be assessed unless the possibilities for interaction among its several
controlling variables acting concurrently were realized; this is what is
different between the laboratory and the real world. In the laboratory,
variables are made to act "one at a time" for all practical purposes. The real
world simply puts the environment back together again. Multiple causality
is never mentioned in the review; it is mentioned throughout *Verbal
Behavior.* The mystery of its omission from the review is compounded by
the fact that Chomsky found it mysterious that Skinner thought something
so complex as speech could be accounted for "by a simple function"!

But the review, however approximate, had an enormous influence in psychology. Nearly every aspect of currently popular psycholinguistic dogma
was adumbrated in it, including its warlike tone; the new look is a frown. It
speaks of itself as a "revolution," not as a research area; it produces "confrontations," not inquiries. So far there have been no telling engagements
in the revolution. The declaration of war has been unilateral, probably
because the behaviorist cannot clearly recognize why he should defend
himself. He has not hurt anyone; he has not preempted the verbal territory
by applying his methods to verbal behavior; he has not used up all of the
verbal behavior nor has he precluded other scientists from investigating it
to their heart's content, with any methods and theories which please them;
he need not be routed before they do so.[8]

VI   Babies and Students in Boxes

In addition to confounding pigeons and people, Skinner has been accused of insulting babies and teachers by trying to make them more efficient. Because babies are meant to grow and prosper, Skinner sought means to encourage their prosperous growth. Because teachers are meant to instruct, Skinner proposed a technology of instructing. To facilitate the production of better babies and better students, Skinner designed new apparatus. First he invented a "baby-box," a piece of apparatus in which the temperature, humidity, and other aspects of the environment important to the welfare of an infant can be controlled. There need be no dimunition in parental love, he reasoned, just because the care of certain needs of an infant are turned over to an efficient mechanical device designed to protect the little one from the essentially hostile environment of uncontrolled Nature. The kind of anxiety Kierkegaard, for example, defined as the human condition, does not benefit an infant intent on survival. Skinner preferred to assure a child adequate food, comfortable temperatures, and safety from attack.

When Skinner began to propagandize for an improved technology of teaching, he assumed that eventually educators would cooperate and define teaching rather than attack his use of the word technology. If, of course, teaching has no ascertainable content and thus no definable methodology, a technology of teaching logically need not be feared. It could never exist. If, however, teachers know what they want to teach, that is, in what ways they want to alter the behavior of their students, then they should be concerned and accountable. If they can define their task they might be able to perform it efficiently.

When Skinner asserted that teachers themselves often seemed not to profit from experience, he was attacking neither their curricula nor their good intentions. He was describing an observed confusion between behavior and implied goals. Immediately he was accused of wanting to reduce teachers to machines as well as intending to elevate machines to teachers. A teaching machine, however, is only a device for providing positive reinforcement of an elementary sort. It usefully supplements and facilitates the kind of live teaching that can articulate its intentions. A product of human ingenuity, it is cleverly but not deceptively rigged to respond to human behavior. Most importantly, the machine is always under the control of those live people who program, adjust, and evaluate its performance. It is neither a robot nor a monster.

In all fairness, however, any defense of programmed instruction must be based on facts about learning. Programming as such implies no values beyond effectiveness. If ineffectiveness is *per se* of higher value, then *efficient* programming is always bad, and theoretically, *inefficiency* should be efficiently encouraged. Programmed instruction, in any case, is frankly behavioristic in its assumption that behavior can be changed by reinforcing desired alterations in what the student is doing. Reassuring a student by a machine or by a teacher that he is correct at any given moment in what he is saying or doing is demonstrably reinforcing, and thus the student learns whatever the machine or the teacher is programmed to teach him.

Most programmed instruction breaks down the material to be taught into small steps. Each step is then reinforced separately. Anything that can be verbalized, Skinner has claimed, is amenable to mechanical teaching. Although the machine handles the programmed text in various ways, it exploits the principles of the original Skinner box in which the rat was encouraged to press a lever under various conditions. Usually the student is not confined to an austere box but he is encouraged to relate to an apparatus: that is, his attention is directed to the limited environment represented by the machine.

In one model of a teaching machine correct answers appear in a window on the front of the apparatus. The student compares his answer with the machine's answer. His pleasure at having made a match reinforces him and he is likely to repeat the pleasing performance later. Obviously the machine itself is innocent; however, insofar as the machine can replace the mechanical chores which formerly burdened live teachers—who got paid for being so burdened—its use does have economic implications. Also, of course, it has philosophical and aesthetic implications.

Skinner was interested in what William James once told a group of teachers: "You make a great mistake," James said, "a very great mistake, if you think that psychology, being the science of the mind's laws, is something from which you can deduce definite programs and schemes and methods of instruction for immediate schoolroom use. Psychology is a science, and teaching is an art; and sciences never generate arts directly out of themselves. An intermediatory inventive mind must make the application, by using its originality."[9] William James, however, appears now to have been more of a philosopher and a theologian than a scientist. It is not surprising, given such strong endorsements of teaching as a mysterious, creative art, that many teachers still protest that they are not "mere" technicians. It is equally not surprising that most teachers are underpaid, for artists are notoriously impecunious. Furthermore, students themselves have been conditioned to reinforce the kind of teaching which in turn reinforces students for not learning.

When Skinner defined teaching in *The Technology of Teaching* as "simply the arrangement of contingencies of reinforcement," he was distinguishing planned teaching from hit-and-miss events. "Left to himself in a given environment a student will learn," Skinner wrote, "but he will not necessarily have been taught. The school of experience is no school at all, not because no one learns in it, but because no one teaches. Teaching is the expediting of learning: a person who is taught learns more quickly than one who is not."[10] The old "trial and error" method is inefficient. Neither are students taught by exhorting them to "think," although all learning has presupposed teachers and students and an arrangement between them. Not interested in polemics, Skinner moved directly to the technology of shaping human behavior, a technology based on observable results of varying those arrangements.

For Skinner, there is no autonomous inner-child in the student who accepts or rejects information. Learning is alteration in the student's behavior, and what is learned appears as *new* behavior. Teachers are the agents, as it were, for altering that behavior. Agreeing that the value of competences may vary but that it is always good to know how to do most things, Skinner broke down big competences into small units which could be reinforced separately. In each case, the reinforcement is contingent upon "success." Since "being wrong" leads to aversive consequences, and since aversive consequences are nonreinforcing, Skinner sought to maximize the frequency of positive reinforcements. Concerned with how to program the material to be taught, he took a long, cool look at traditional hit-and-miss teaching and was dismayed at the sight. He attributed the prevalent resistance to improvement, and particularly to technical aids, to "a general fear of power." "Educators," he concluded, "are seldom willing to concede that they are engaged in the control of human behavior."[11] The issue is certainly timely. Unfortunately, "control" is still a bad word.

VII   *Psychotics in Boxes*

Inevitably Skinner and his students expanded their observations and experiments to include psychotic behavior. As early as 1956 Skinner modestly reported the results of a research project carried out at the Metropolitan State Hospital at Waltham, Massachusetts, noting at the time that he had spent relatively little of his professional life working with psychotics and therefore he was not identifying himself as a "specialist" in psychiatry.[12] Because, however, he reasonably enough considered psychotic behavior to be real behavior, he felt qualified to work with "patients" in a hospital. In his report of the 1956 experiments Skinner necessarily emphasized the rationale, for at that time the behaviorist's approach to illness seemed superficial to clinicians researching the mental content of patients' verbalizations as the most cogent evidence of their troubles and thus the most effective signposts to a possible cure. Rejecting ideologically as well as pragmatically the reality of unconscious events in anyone and working only with the patient's observable responses, Skinner first put the patient in a box—"a small pleasant room." He limited the patient's environment for several hours a day to a controlled situation, although the sick person was never coerced to enter the "box" nor to stay in it longer than he wished. The room was furnished with a chair and a device similar to a vending machine, with a button or a plunger that could be operated to satisfy the patient's momentary needs by the inserting of an adequate coin in an appropriate slot.

Skinner observed that many psychotics who had been diagnosed as unable to care for themselves could learn to operate such a vending machine—could learn, that is, to act productively on the environment when reinforced for properly inserting tokens for the candy, cigarettes or food the machine could eject, or for pleasantly colored pictures the machine could project on a screen. Skinner did *not* enthusiastically announce that all psychotics could be cured by learning to operate vending machines. The *facts* were reported, the implications suggested. So-called normal behavior differs from so-called psychotic behavior in its effectiveness and in its appearance. People who *seem* to be behaving sanely are said to be sane, and people who are said to be sane are treated by others as if they were sane without regard to fictions about motives. A person who knows how to satisfy his appetites by using tokens to obtain desired merchandise, is behaving sanely.

At the time, Skinner hoped for spectacular results. "It is not inconceivable," he speculated, "that the mental apparatus and all that it implies will be forgotten. It will then be more than a mere working hypothesis to say . . . that psychotic behavior, like all behavior, is part of the world of observable events to which the powerful methods of natural science apply and to the understanding of which they will prove adequate."[13] For some sick people to learn to behave as efficiently as a healthy chimp would be a real advance toward sanity. Achieving immediate results instead of consulting a philosopher's table on long-term values has been customary in the clinic. Both electric shock therapy and chemical therapy have looked first to results and only secondarily to explanatory processes. Behaviorism, however, looks to both, and thus its case is strengthened. Some men may not go gently into the Skinner box. They may rage, rage against the reinforcement schedule, but it is possible that there is no other choice.

CHAPTER 5

What Man Can Make of Man: Beyond Freedom and Dignity

IN science all conclusions are tentative. The scientist draws no final line under a column of facts. There is no Grand Total. Most importantly, the future stretches infinitely ahead, full of enough time to know everything. In 1971 Skinner asserted that the "evolution of a culture is a gigantic exercise in self-control. It is often said that a scientific view of man leads to wounded vanity, a sense of hopelessness, and nostalgia. But no theory changes what it is a theory about; man remains what he has always been. And a new theory may change what can be done with its subject matter. A scientific view of man offers exciting possibilities. We have not yet seen what man can make of man."[1]

The existentialist philosopher tells of man's anxiety and teaches that an irreducible amount of that anxiety defines the human condition; nevertheless, he feels uneasy about the discrepancy between things as they are and as they might be if man would act to change them. Although to such a philosopher man is free, he is free because the universe is indifferent to him and not because he has willed his freedom. The behavioral scientist also tells of man's anxiety but he stresses the possibility as well as the desirability of reducing that anxiety. Above all, he does not exalt philosophical Absurdity. Although he denies that his subject matter is free to change *at will*, he may also *feel* sad about the indifference of the universe. The establishing of discrepancies between things as they are and things as they might be is for him, however, not a glory but a challenge. His science acknowledges no irreducible discrepancies. His resistance to Absurdity, then, is expressed in his daily resistance to small absurdities, to ignorance, and to superstition. In a way, without exalting heroism he may act more heroically than the existentialist, for whatever he does is in full knowledge that his choices are not really free choices and that his reasonableness—if any—is a function of

90

the existence of an ultimate lawfulness and not of his will to be reasonable. For him the real miracle is that there are no miracles because there is no need for them. Lawful reality is awesome enough.

I *Behavioral Grace*

While many philosophers have been charged with not spelling out the way to a better life, Skinner in contrast, has been charged with spelling it out all too soon and all too clearly. Before the untimely death of Albert Camus, for example, some of the philosopher's admirers thought they had detected signs of their master's imminent return to Christianity. They hoped Camus would finally "save them." Fallen men might again become Christians and properly contrite and thus candidates for a newly activated God's grace. In contrast, Skinner offers an easy solution. Skinner's behaving man is never *necessarily* contrite, and the only grace possible to a behavioral scientist qua scientist is strictly secular and is manifested as further discoveries of demonstrable functional relationships. That grace, however, is available to everyone.

Skinner has claimed that his functional analysis of behavior avoids most value problems. His analysis of the behavior of people in groups, behavior traditionally considered the province of sociology and social psychology, is a logical extension of his analysis of the behavior of rats, pigeons, and human laboratory subjects. Thus Skinner essentially sees each person as an organism being controlled by, and in turn countercontrolling, other organisms. Skinner's program implies little need for the specialized disciplines of anthropology and sociology. To Skinner the kinds and degrees of control set up by the social situation follow the same arrangements observed in the behavior of organisms in which the reinforcement is provided by the mechanical universe. Thus in his analysis of "social institutions" Skinner moves easily from the observed behavior of a single organism to the more complex behavior under the control of institutions.

An institution for Skinner is a group of people behaving in specifiable ways under identifiable controls. Because the controls, such as money and praise, are identifiable even if often subtle, Skinner "accounts for" the existence of most social institutions as examples of operant conditioning. Wide and deep implications of behavior modification of humans by other humans emerge when that modification is "engineered" through operant conditioning rather than induced by moral laws or coerced by physical force. Experimentation with operant conditioning as a means to a better world made up of socially useful and fulfilled people has accelerated since Skinner's radical denial of traditional "freedom" and "dignity" as either necessary or sufficient coordinates of *feeling* free and *living* with dignity. The passing years have borne witness to increasing support of divergent ideas about what man can make of man. So strongly conditioned, however, is the fear of being conditioned, that the controversy often bogs down in a semantic nightmare. Fear of "control" is extended to fear of all names associated with automation. The alleged horrors of automation, however, have little to do directly with Skinner or with behavioral science, for many machines have been useful and defended by humanists. Since the wheel and lever were invented, machines have been helpful devices in all societies. It is as useless to indict a machine per se as it is to punish the mechanic. The nexus to attack, if any, is the functional relationship between the product and the producer.

The machine as the villain in the drama is a poor antagonist. A product of man's ingenuity, the machine has no essence beyond what the programmer gives it. The charge against Skinner that he conceives of man as a computer to be programmed is a metaphysical conceit which despite its dramatic appeal is not very sensible. All science uses computers. So-called errors are corrected impersonally and thus with impunity by machines, whereas prophets have often been killed for attempting to eradicate simple errors in social planning. Mathematical manipulations, for example, are conveniently relegated to a machine: everyone knows how fallible humans can be when adding, dividing, or subtracting numbers. Glorifying that human fallibility as the essence of humanity emphasizes the irony of a primitive faith in humans merely because they are not mechanically efficient. Knowledge is not necessarily fatal to man's glory. When all poets know that the nightingale sings to proclaim its territorial rights rather than to praise God, poetry will not necessarily disappear. Poets who know things may be the better for their knowledge and able to address themselves to the tension between what is known and what is felt without confounding the two.

Skinner's knowledge has always included his knowing about how others feel about his behaviorism. Yet his audacious vision has continued to project an inexorably reasonable extrapolation from what he knows to what might be done with what he knows. In the latter part of his career he has gracefully accepted the inevitable problems as well as the pleasures of being B. F. Skinner.

In 1967 Skinner told Mary Harrington Hall of *Psychology Today* that if his significance was to be "limited to just one thing, it would be the whole question of the contingencies of reinforcement arranged by schedules of reinforcement and their role in the analysis of operant behavior." Then Skinner went on to deplore the fact that "nobody pays much attention to it at all." Later in the same interview, in a slightly different context, Skinner lamented the fact that among his contemporaries, he could "mention only one or two who really very seriously changed their attitudes toward the study of behavior as a result of anything I have ever done or said." He went on, however, to predict that younger psychologists would be affected. When Mary Hall rightfully identified this prediction as "optimistic about the future of operant conditioning" Skinner emphatically agreed, for in his opinion, based on fact, of course, "there really isn't much competition for the allegiance of bright and informed young psychologists."[2]

In 1968 Skinner told another interviewer, Richard I. Evans, how he felt about his career: "As I look back on it, it seems to me that two important things were the use of rate of responding as a basic datum and the so-called cumulative record which makes changes in rate conspicuous." When asked to "look to the future," Skinner revealed his new area of concern as "the kinds of opposition one encounters when trying to apply a science of behavior to human betterment." Thus Evans was able to conclude that after all "Dr. Skinner appears to be essentially a humanist in the most straightforward connotation of this term. This is evidenced by his concern with eliminating aversive control in society, his optimism concerning man's capability for dealing with his most difficult problems, and his staunch belief in the basic potential of *all* men for a 'good life' regardless of their deficits in so-called measured intelligence and their so-called emotional limitations."[3]

II   *Behaviorism Comes of Age*

In 1969 Skinner published various essays, lectures, and papers gathered together under the title *Contingencies of Reinforcement*.[4] The volume represents a readable cross section of the more controversial issues in Skinnerian behaviorism in the late 1960s, the period which marks the escalation of Skinner's interest in phylogeny. In order to explain *all* behavior Skinner refers in his

1969 work to two sets of contingencies: phylogenic and ontogenic. The former "are responsible for the fact that men respond to stimuli, act upon the environment, and change their behavior under contingencies of reinforcement."[5] They "explain" the survival of the species. "All human behavior, including the behavior of the machines which man builds to behave in his place," Skinner now boldly asserts, "is ultimately to be accounted for in terms of the phylogenic contingencies of survival which have produced man as a species and the ontogenic contingencies of reinforcement which have produced him as an individual" (297). He does, however, make a distinction between "rule-governed" and "contingency-shaped" behavior. For Skinner "machines are law-abiding citizens; they always follow the rules." The charge that machines will always remain inferior to men unless purposiveness can be built into the machine is countered by Skinner by rejecting *all* intentionality—in men and in machines. Purpose, Skinner insists, is not a "characteristic or essence of the topography of behavior." It is only a "relation to controlling variables" (291).

A machine capable of behavior as complex as that of a human organism would not *know* it is a machine. It would, in fact, be a human being. So perhaps perfected machines already exist as potentiated persons, not recognized as such by their inferiors—humanoids or computers. Machines capable of responding to ontogenic contingencies would have come through their own phylogeny! The conjecture seems to belong to "science fiction" (properly renamed lately "speculative fiction") but is not logically inept in a Skinnerian context. In any event, in 1971 Skinner chose the most controversial title possible for the first of his mature summation-defense books—*Beyond Freedom and Dignity*.[6]

With a farewell glance at some of his own youthful hopes and fears, in this controversial work Skinner rejects the labels "dignity" and "freedom" and opts instead for their psychological equivalents. He attacks the theory that man will never "accept the fact that he can be controlled" (164). He counterattacks what he calls "literature of freedom," detecting "signs of emotional instability in those who have been deeply affected by the literature" (165). Answering the charge that "the scientific analysis of human behavior was responsible for the assassinations of John and Robert Kennedy," Skinner refers the event to behavioral rather than moral coordinates: "If any theory is to be blamed it is the all but universal theory of a free and worthy autonomous man" (167).

Skinner's emphasis on behavior had always been abrasive even to the most generous humanists, but this new manifesto alerted the pack. The defenders of freedom and dignity began to demonstrate the very discrepancy between verbal behavior and other behavior (what dictator has not set out to *free* his people?) that Skinner had observed and commented on. Skinner's mere articulation of the fact that "freedom" and "dignity" had been abused lost him some of his last humanist friends. Did he *want* hostile reactions in order to promote absurd rejoinders which would demonstrate to astute and objective observers just how predictably irrational his hostile critics were becoming? Such a possibility suggests a Machiavellianism that is foreign to the personality of "Fred" Skinner. It is not, however, inconceivable.

A democracy traditionally protects the "freedom" of one individual to get ahead of another. In this context, Skinner cites a critical case in the uses and abuses of leisure. The claim that it is good to be free to do nothing is merely vague verbalizing. Leisure, operationally defined, is having nothing to do—with the emphasis on the nothing. Skinner's argument is ingenious. He cites the variable-ratio schedule of reinforcement as the explanation of *how* certain habits are established in leisure as a function of ordinary weak reinforcements that the leisure itself has strengthened! "When strong reinforcers are no longer effective, lesser reinforcers take over" (178). Voicing the *words* "freedom" and "dignity" acts as a reinforcer to members of the leisure class. At the same time, the *facts* about freedom and dignity—that is, free and dignified *behavior*—have become weaker and weaker general reinforcers. For example, well-off people who do not have to work for a living have more time and thus better means to protect their dignified holdings and their free status from the threats of those who have neither time nor means. Inevitably the verbalizations of the latter about how good it would be to be "free" and "dignified" are reinforced by those who have something to gain by defending the words "freedom" and "dignity." If freedom from the need to work gives one the dignity to use all one's time in the pursuit of art, music, and litertature, and if such pursuits are the highest good, then no decent person should object to reinforcing leisure for others as well as for himself. "Doing as one pleases" seems to many people to be good, but whether the doing or the saying of it is more reinforcing is problematic. Wealthy people who apparently have gained dignity and freedom reinforce the laboring of others by hiring them and then complimenting them on how well they do what they have been hired to do as well as paying them. For Skinner the survival of a culture is threatened by its own *verbalized* values unless those values are also activated and thus made reinforcing to the *whole* group. Leisure is not, in fact, an unequivocal good: "Leisure is one of the great challenges to those who are concerned with the survival of a culture because any attempt to control what a person does when he does not need to do anything is particularly likely to be attacked as unwarranted meddling" (180).

Because Skinner could predict hostile responses from those who were reinforced for defending freedom and dignity—at any level—he needed to distinguish between good and bad substitutes for "freedom." Noting that any "misuse of a technology of behavior is a serious matter," he suggested that such a miscarriage could be avoided "by looking not at putative controllers but at the contingencies under which they control. It is not the benevolence of a controller but the contingencies under which he controls benevolently which must be examined. All control is reciprocal, and an interchange between control and countercontrol is essential to the evolution of a culture. The interchange is disturbed by the literatures of freedom and dignity, which interpret countercontrol as the suppression rather than the correction of controlling practices" (182 - 83).

The attempt to "control" control, as it were, with countercontrol rather than with either freedom or suppression is a neat ploy and much more semantically sophisticated than anti-Skinnerians could see. If it were true that human beings could live better with *no* controls upon them and still survive—that is, if they could live without habits and adjustments and learned values—then the elimination of all controls would be reinforcing. The denunciation of all controls, however, is in fact only a special kind of control: namely, a plea that is differentially reinforcing (usually as words) to special groups previously conditioned to feel less anxiety when they are told they are "free." Eventually, of course, the issue narrows down to the difference between good and bad controls rather than between controls or no controls, for nothing except chaos is free. Fortunately, "good" and "bad" are definable with reference to survival value. Those who find this parameter too narrow or otherwise distasteful must then in all fairness disprove Skinner's contentions by improving society without invoking controls. To do so, of course, would require, at least at first, the stringent control of all would-be controllers.[7]

III   *Behaviorism as Philosophy*

"Behaviorism is not the science of human behavior: it is the philosophy of that science."[8] Thus in 1974 Skinner boldly introduces his second summation-defense book, *About Behaviorism*, which is both a primer about behaviorism and an apology for his career. Confessing that in his maturity he does not necessarily approve of the behavior of all who call themselves behaviorists, the master sets out, finally it would seem, to extract from his own work and that of his followers a more or less systematic philosophy, something which has been implicit in his later research but never before spelled out.

Skinner confronts his subject head-on: "Here, for example, are some of the things commonly said about behaviorism or the science of behavior. They are all, I believe, wrong" (3 - 4). Among the misunderstandings about behaviorism he lists twenty items which he intends to correct. Convinced that he is right, Skinner gives fair warning in *About Behaviorism* that he is not only explaining his philosophy but also defending his science. "The major problems facing the world today," he boldly asserts, "can be solved only if we improve our understanding of human behavior" (8). His conviction is less arrogant than compassionate. The crisis which in good faith he believes can be resolved does really exist. Skinner's urgency is grounded in concern. To one who knows that mere telling about something will not per se change much, such telling is existentially heroic. "Traditional views have been around for centuries," he coolly observes, "and I think it is fair to say that they have proved to be inadequate" (8). Skinner also knows, however, that the persistence of these traditional views must have been reinforcing, and that despite their inadequacy they cannot be extinguished by logical argument. Nevertheless, with the dignity he had seemed to reject, and *apparently* of his own free will, Skinner finally promotes, like a thoughtful evangelist, the program he "believes" in. His heroism is nonetheless heroic for being somewhat absurd—absurd because he is right!

By 1974 Skinner is able to deny strenuously that his behaviorism "ignores consciousness, feelings, and states of mind" (4). This acceptance of the reality-status of inwardnesses is dramatic news to those who remember early behaviorism's austere insistence on empty organisms. He also now denies that behaviorism rejects innate endowment, that it reduces people to robots, that it neglects cognition, intention, purpose, creative achievements, the self and the sense of self, the mind, and personality. (He yields nothing of his science, however, for he can still transform these concepts into behavioral ones.) He rejects all implications that behaviorism neglects people in favor of rats and that its laboratory methods are so restrictive and its philosophy so reductive that its truths cannot be referred to "daily life." He challenges all the familiar indictments of behaviorism. Aware of the fact that the behavioral scientist is himself perforce as conditioned and as predictable as the subjects in his laboratory, he denies that *that* fact invalidates his position. He insists that behaviorism need not be dehumanizing or "indifferent to the warmth and richness of human life [or] . . . incompatible with the creation and enjoyment of art, music, and literature, and with love for one's fellowmen" (5).

Beginning the demonstration of the validity of his philosophy with nontechnical explanations of what behavioral psychologists have been doing in labs and clinics, Skinner necessarily often stoops to the vernacular. Although he still prefers to assign "the causes of behavior" to observables only, in the interest of communication with a general reader he patiently translates the fictions of mentalism into behavioral terms rather than dismissing them as unscientific. Although mentalism was bad because it "kept attention away from the external antecedent events which might have explained behavior, by seeming to supply an alternative explanation," it is no longer necessary to reject the reality of private awareness. Skinner's radical behaviorism in its sophisticated stage "does not insist upon truth by agreement and can therefore consider events taking place in the private world within the skin. It does not call these events unobservable, and it does not dismiss them as subjective. It simply questions the nature of the object observed and the reliability of the observations" (16 - 17).

Skinner's acceptance of the reality of an "inner man" does not, however, imply his approval of "consciousness" and "mind" as behavioral realities. What a person "feels" and "thinks" are *causes* of behavior only insofar as emotion and thought are bodily events. A person's body may be part of a person's environment, but introspection is not a reliable method for physiological research. Scientific rigor is not compromised, however, when the behaviorist moves inside the organism and recognizes *reports* of feelings and so-called ideas (i.e., self-knowledge) as legitimate data as long as the reports are dealt with as behavior rather than as infallible "meanings."

Easily observable behavior, such as drinking a glass of water, can be checked on by others, so that if a person *says* he is drinking water while *in fact* he can also be observed to be so doing, the person is credited with telling the truth. But headaches and other inner events are more difficult to check on. What a person *says*, of course, has always been considered significant data by behaviorists, but no assumption about the relationship between the report and inner states may be taken for granted. The scientist must not leap to faith in the credibility of what his subject *says*. The scientist never overlooks the distinction between a truly private feeling and the public report of that feeling, even in subjects trying to be honest. He also knows, however, that his subject sometimes knows how the subject feels—that there is, at least for the subject, such a "thing" as self-knowledge. Because Skinner still insists that this kind of knowledge is conditioned rather than innate, he has not really yielded much either to mentalists or moralists who defend human autonomy as a function of the mind (or soul) and thus the responsibility of all human beings.

A concept like "instinct," for example, explains nothing. It merely describes—redundantly, at that. To call nest building instinctive does not account for the behavior. It merely indicates the fact that most birds build nests. "A more serious mistake is made in converting an instinct into a force" (35), writes Skinner. To assume that animals attack *because* they possess aggressive instincts, begs the question, Skinner asserts. "The attack is the only evidence we have of the tendency to attack" (36). By now it is clear that Skinner sees the so-called attack as either learned behavior or behavior that has guaranteed survival, that is, in any case, an event upon which survival of the individual and the species has been contingent. Contingencies of survival which Skinner believes are beyond reasonable doubt, although difficult to experiment with, include mating, caring for the young, and defenses against predators. Also, certain conditions inside the body make it more or less likely that the body will survive. These conditions are internal environments, and they function just as any feature of the external environment does in reinforcing survival behavior.

Skinner emphasizes once again how operant conditioning accounts for subtleties of behavior otherwise not explicable. Although he notes that the two kinds of conditioning, operant and instrumental, parallel the two kinds of behavior unscientifically called voluntary and involuntary, there is still neither place nor need for "will" in Skinner's philosophy, and certainly not in his science. Although operant behavior *seems* to the behaving person to be more nearly under his personal control, and reflexive behavior, such as Pavlov developed in his dogs, *seems* to be under outside controls or even invading spirits, Skinner asserts more confidently than ever that only two sets of contingencies, contingencies of survival and contingencies of reinforcement, adequately account for all the intricate performances of any organism, including humans—given, of course, the genetic determinants.

Skinner claims he can also explain intention, introspection, and creativity adequately without either denying that such abstractions are meaningful to lay people of good will or capitulating to the elaborate defense of such terms by cognition-psychologists. Survival behavior, traditionally denoted as instinctive, and truly new forms of behavior traditionally exalted as creative, are in Skinner's philosophy always generated rather than willed. The imitative behavior of a newborn duckling, for example, who follows the mother duck around, has survival value for the young ones. The behavior is referred by Skinner to the duckling's "capacity to be reinforced by maintaining or reducing the distance between itself and a moving object" (41). The duckling can be conditioned to behave in the same way with respect to objects other than its biological mother. It can also be taught to move away from such objects—a disastrous lesson! The behaviorist's philosophical position *vis-a-vis* the human being is just as skeptical of anything more mysterious than an inherited capacity to learn how to survive. "It begins and remains a biological system, and the behavioristic position is that it is nothing more than that" (44).

Modern behaviorism, by translating the vocabulary of "feelings" and "thoughts" into descriptions of behavior controlled by environmental factors interacting with genetic endowments, still remains dispassionate. Skinner's definition of love, for example, is coolly behavioristic: "With respect to a person with whom we interact . . . to 'love' is to behave in ways having certain kinds of effects, possibly with accompanying conditions which may be felt" (49). Love does not *cause* one to behave in certain ways. Love *is* that behavior.

Traditional virtues and ideals are also brought down to the earthiness of behavioral specifications. Bravery is not necessarily virtuous, and happiness is not necessarily trivial; both, however, are often indistinguishable from ignoble qualities when defined behaviorally. Bravery and foolishness, for example, are quite similar. "A fool," according to Skinner, "rushes into a dangerous situation not because he feels reckless but because reinforcing consequences have completely offset punishing . . ." (64). A brave act and a foolish one are both controlled by the kind of reinforcement which the community uses to offset obvious risks. Happiness is a by-product of operant conditioning rather than a definable goal or specific act. Anxiety is reinforced when the community is building up the kind of foolishness called bravery. The fact that people are capable of so-called imaginative behavior has never been denied by Skinner, for he knows better than most that the human organism "may see things when there is nothing to be seen . . ." (85). That indisputable fact led, Skinner concluded, to the invention of "mind" as the control over the imagination.

Imagination, which was once believed too subtle a concept for behaviorism, is only a vague term for the organism's ability to discriminate between seeing what is not there and seeing what is there. The awake, sane organism has learned the difference between the so-called imagined and the so-called real. The dreaming or schizophrenic organism, however, does not "know" the difference between dreaming and hallucinating at the time it is dreaming or hallucinating. Although some introspective knowledge that it is dreaming may be present at the time—or some awareness of being insane—that knowledge or awareness is weak. When the knowledge is strong, the organism is truly awake and sane. These apparent capitulations to the reality of self-knowledge do not imply, however, that Skinner finally accepts the reality of "mind" as the metaphysical manifestation of a brain. Man's mind is an abstraction derived from his behavior, and thinking occurs only as behavior similar to running, although the former is certainly less available for direct observation than the latter. "The history of human thought," Skinner concludes harmlessly enough, "is what people have said and done" (117).

With considerable poise Skinner accepts the reality of an *apparent* freedom-of-choice in humans without compromising his commitment to determinism. "To exercise a choice," Skinner explains, "is simply to act, and the choice a person is capable of making is the act itself" (113). Freedom to act otherwise does not, of course, exist. Any assumption that one could behave other than the way he is behaving at the moment refers to the whole paradigm rather than that moment. Obviously, had one's genetic-endowment and reinforcement history been different, one would have *had* to act differently.

The most abrasive criticisms of behaviorism are directed toward its skepticism of the roles assigned traditionally to reasoning and choosing. The behaviorist has observed that although so-called decisions are frequently both unreasonable and thoughtless, they nevertheless persist unless the behaving organism is reconditioned. It is also a fact that unreasonable actions are sometimes effective. The mature Skinner is surer than ever that contingencies account for all these deviations from reason and that even much admired virtues are controlled by the *consequences* of behavior. Skinner asks a therapist, for example, to understand that the *cause* of his patient's aberrant behavior is to be found in the relationship between his behavior and its results on his environment rather than in the patient's mind. "Cognitive input," for example, seems to Skinner a pretentious name for something that may occur in reality but which will be effective only to the extent that contingencies are arranged to insure reinforcement.

Other traditionally positive values are easily if not happily translated into behavioral terms. "Faith," according to Skinner, "is a matter of the strength of behavior resulting from contingencies which have not been analyzed" (133). Resolving "reason" into behavior, Skinner rejects "cognitive input" as well as a "trans-rational region of the mind." Yet he insists on the usefulness of the concept traditionally called "intuition" or "instinct" as "the very starting point of a behavioral analysis" (132). The point is well made, for intuitionists also reject rationalism and its ethical abstractions. Intuitive behavior does exist—in the sense of behavior under the control of unidentifiable factors, and also as well-reinforced social habits—"the behavior we possess by virtue of the practices of our verbal community" (132).

IV   *Innocent or Guilty?*

Skinner's assertions about human behavior and the research which underwrites those assertions are now available for evaluating and testing to those who can understand them. It is well to remember, however, that understanding is not always easy to achieve. Einstein's relativity theories, for example, are not completely available to anyone except sophisticated mathematicians. Perhaps that is why Einstein has been less feared and hated than Skinner. In contrast, Skinner's clear prose deceives even the uninformed into assuming they "understand" behaviorism. Almost everyone who can read has an opinion about *that Skinner!* Despite concessions to nonspecialists in the summing up of his position in *About Behaviorism,* Skinner clearly remains the undaunted champion of the importance of the environment. That very clarity arouses hostility. Demonstrating the futility of urging people to reform by an act of will, Skinner seems to exhort his reader to act willfully at least once: to freely give up his freedom. Skinner says that man cannot become the master of his fate without manipulating his environment. Thus in asking others to endorse his kind of intellectual and ethical self-management Skinner is really pleading that they *choose* to analyze the contingencies outside themselves as well as *choose* to apply rules based on past experiences. He *seems* for a moment to deny his assumption that no one is *really* free to choose. The apparent inconsistency comes from the fact that before Skinner events inside the organism were not classified as anything other than innate—that is, as nonenvironmental and thus the *real* self. In his urgency Skinner would have us derive new and better rules from both analyses and experiments by informing us of the facts—the only truly behavioral way of communicating. Yet in our urgency we *have* to rely partially on unproved folk wisdom and nonexperimental folkways in the interim. Although our cultural heritage, unfortunately, is cluttered with useless and even dangerous artifacts, it is also quite real—and above all, for better or for worse, it has survived.

That human beings—as a species—have survived is also a fact for now, and Skinner finds that an agreeable fact. He fears, however, that survival is not a birthright. When Skinner asks human beings to engineer survival, to do something about it, he is using ordinary discourse, but in the lab he defines that "doing something" as a series of arbitrations between man and nature which will or will not lead to survival. First we must find out how "it" may be done, and then we must proceed to *do* "it," outfacing the paradox that man is simultaneously the most vulnerable and the most resourceful of all organisms.

Is Skinner on the side of Satan? Is he tempting us to endorse power without dignity, survival without freedom, and happiness without honor? The analogy is provocative. Satan offered knowledge and power in an attempt to subvert humanity. Skinner offers knowledge and power in an attempt to save humanity. "In the behavioristic view," he says confidently in the closing lines of *About Behaviorism*, "man can now control his own destiny because he knows what must be done and how to do it" (251). Such a reliance on the power of knowledge is without humility but not without grace, at least to those who understand Skinner's commitment.

In 1971 Skinner "made" the cover of an American magazine noted for its alliterative journalese. The cover story exulted in the infamous behaviorist's ability to arouse maximum emotions and said he was "adored as a messiah and abhorred as a menace."[9] Although the rhetoric would seem to divide the pros and cons evenly, the bias of the journalist against Skinner was strongly supported by subsequent reader response to Skinner's picture appearing on the cover of a prestigious stronghold of American morality. In fact, the count showed that Skinner at the time was almost as unpopular as Edward Kennedy, whose recent encounter with his own unfortunate contingencies and aversive stimuli was still fresh in the popular press. The vote came to 354 against Skinner and 71 for him, with Skinner pulling almost twice as many total votes as Kennedy. Such a small sample, of course, did not bother the editors, for statistics are sacred even to antistatisticians when the numbers come out on their side.

In any event, polls of people versus pigeons predictably always favor people, for although Skinner's pigeons have learned to do many unexpectedly intricate things, they do not conduct polls. Although asking a pigeon how it feels about being potentiated has not yet stimulated verbal behavior, conditioned chimps may soon confound humanists with their clever use of symbols and signs and have some "say" about their own lives—may even demand the vote. The point is that utterances are not inherently meaningful. They must be learned and then decoded in contexts. So far, however, the serious implications of Skinner's possible role as messiah or menace, as Savior or Satan, have been obscured in the popular mind, which identifies him with pigeons and rats. He himself, however, has wrestled with his own significance in several book-length products of his maturity as scientist and—if one may use the "tact" that Skinner once himself forbade—as *thinker*. The fear, however, of anything that might work is understandable, and when Skinner is feared by those who know how much he does know, that fear is more significant than the quick prejudices of the uninformed. To be judged by those who know is far different from being condemned by those who do not know. In the latter case it makes little sense to speak of being judged, for the evidence has not been allowed into court, so polls may be dismissed as trivial.

At this time and in this place evidence is available for fair judges and fair juries to evaluate. Certainly Skinner did assume during the bad days of World War II that "we" must win. Although he has not continued to endorse aggressive nationalism he believes that "society" can be saved. His increasing interest in experimental communities is realistic and is a response to the need for trying alternatives to today's failed cities. Thus he has inadvertently seemed to direct his concerns more and more into the messianic role. Yet his professional life is now rounding off; for when any man starts to write his full-length autobiography he has, by definition, admitted to viewing his life as choreographed and clearly enough performed for him to assess the success of his choreography-become-his-dance.

Each of Skinner's most significant group of achievements, first reported in articles and essays, eventually led to a proper book. His doctoral dissertation, for example, became *The Behavior of Organisms*. After his experiments and extrapolations led to further refinements on the doings of his first operantly operating rat, *Walden Two* and its textbook counterpart, *Science and Human Behavior* appeared, followed by *Verbal Behavior* and other books on the facts and implications of operant conditioning in schools and society. After his careful analysis in 1969 of various contingencies of reinforcement, which he qualified in the subtitle as a *theoretical* analysis, the way was open and the time happily available for writing two more partially theoretical manifestos—each one, in a sense, the complement of the other. Skinner's attempt to inform the world that freedom and dignity have become useless words at best, and dangerous shibboleths in the hands of exploiters at worst, infuriated those who had been becoming more and more uncomfortable about this new prophet.

Perhaps to reassure his enemies that they were not wrong in fearing him, Skinner followed up with a less violent but nevertheless strongly committed book. *About Behaviorism* is a kind of a summing up but far from an all-passion-spent epilogue. Although the mature behaviorist now used familiar words instead of behavioral jargon part of the time, and although he gladly admitted that "awareness" can be said to exist, and even accepted certain ways of handling "motives" and "ideas," his invitation to meet in the middle of a bridge, as it were, between humanism and behaviorism was not immediately responded to by many. Yet the metaphor of a bridge has been heuristic in more than one respect. Satan, according to certain authorities whose facts have not often been subjected to magazine polls, once built a bridge between earth and hell for *his* subverts to travel. Because Satan's profession was sincerely destructive, his bridge was a one-way affair. It seems not unreasonable to conclude that Skinner has also been trying to build a bridge between humanism, represented by the literature and music he has always valued, and his radical behaviorism. His bridge, perforce, would run two ways, so that possible converts and subverts could travel in either direction, for *if* the humanists are as free as they claim to be, they need not be subverted. They could always return with their dignity intact after investigating Skinner's side of the putative chasm between their style and his. And if the Skinnerians, although strong converts as they seem to be, become uncomfortable on Skinner's side, predictably they would no longer be reinforced and the habit of being a Skinnerian would be extinguished, and they could return "home."

Bridges, however, sometimes collapse. At best they only span without closing chasms, so that metaphor is a "sloppy tact" and may soon enough fade into another platitude—the certain fate of all once lively metaphysical conceits that become popular. In any event, let the last word here be one that has not, despite centuries of use and misuse, completely faded: Burrhus Frederick Skinner has always been a *gentleman*.

Notes and References

Chapter One

1. *The Behavior of Organisms* (New York, 1938), p. 6. This was Skinner's first book-length study. It is an austere report of the behavior of one rat, the experiment which earned Skinner his doctorate at Harvard and that demonstrated the reality of operant conditioning. Although eventually to become scriptural to Skinnerians, its significance was not immediately apparent to most psychologists.

In contrast to Skinner, another early rat psychologist, Edward Tolman, mixed his science with modesty, humor, and even confusion, and consequently was tolerated more easily. Tolman once labeled his observations "a *rat* psychologist's *rat*iocinations offered free." Tolman, who died in 1959, was known primarily as "a purposive behaviorist." His gentle wit and his apparent tolerance of humanism and rationalism made him less formidable than Skinner. Also, his use of traditional psychological jargon in describing his observations kept him less austere to laymen, who understand such words as "drive" and "appetite."

2. *Behaviorism* (Chicago, 1958), p. 6. This is a "renewed" edition of the 1924 edition. Watson's significance, however, is as a pioneer in the early 1920s, when he stood virtually alone as the advocate of a rigorous science of human behavior.

3. Ibid., p. 11.

4. T. W. Wann, ed., *Behaviorism and Phenomenology: Contrasting Bases for Modern Psychology* (Chicago, 1964), p. 84. Wann prints Skinner's essay along with comments and discussion and other essays by members of a symposium (Carl R. Rogers, Sigmund Koch, R. B. MacLeod, Norman Malcolm, and Michael Scriven) held at Rice University. Koch misjudged the meaning of the symposium: to him it was "the death rattle of behaviorism." Skinner's essay also was printed in *Science* 140 (1964), 951 - 58.

5. *Cumulative Record* (New York, 1961), p. vii. A revised edition of *Cumulative Record* in 1972 benefits from the addition of eighteen more

papers. Skinner did not, however, include the brief explanation of his title in the later edition.

There are few difficulties in Skinner's canon, unlike the bibliographies of poets and novelists. In an orderly progression of reports of his research and full-length books announcing the wider implications of his work, Skinner has kept abreast of himself over many years.

6. Ibid., p. 77. This essay was also published in the *American Psychologist* 40 (1956), 221 - 23.

7. Skinner has always been generous with the facts of his life. My sources here for events relevant to this study are mainly two: "B. F. Skinner . . . An Autobiography," which is reprinted in *Festschrift for B. F. Skinner*, ed., P. B. Davis (New York, 1970), and his recent book-length memoir, *Particulars of My Life* (New York, 1976). The former was first printed in Edwin G. Boring and Gardner Lindzey, eds., *A History of Psychology in Autobiography* (1967), V, 385 - 413. The latter is a delightful survey of Skinner's early years up to his entering Harvard Graduate School to study psychology. Other volumes of this memoir are projected. The quotation here is from page 18 of *Particulars*. (Subsequent page references to this work are cited in parentheses after the quotation.)

8. "B. F. Skinner . . . An Autobiography," in *Festschrift*, p. 9.

9. Ibid.

10. Ibid., pp. 9 - 10.

11. "Has Gertrude Stein a Secret?" *The Atlantic Monthly* 153 (January, 1934), 50 - 57. This article is also reprinted in the 1961 and 1972 editions of *Cumulative Record*. Skinner has enjoyed making irreverent, objective analyses of certain aspects of literature held to be beyond the scientist's ken. I first met Professor Skinner in 1947 when as an instructor of writing I attended the behaviorist's class in "Verbal Behavior" at Columbia University. At first I was shocked by his insistence on rejecting the work of all previous linguists, semanticists, and philosophers. However, I soon experienced a veritable conversion. I saw that it was not only possible to approach literature as behavior but that in fact it was the only sensible way. It may seem incredible to anti-Skinnerians, but B. F. Skinner knew as much about literature and the so-called humanities as any dedicated literateur—with one big difference: he enjoyed knowing what he knew. His use of puns that summer was delightful and heuristic. I learned that all language is multiply "caused" and thus quite simply sets the occasion for equally multiple responses. When Skinner announced that "dental laws," for example, "must have teeth in them" to become effective, I saw *both* his points. I learned that "an unvarnished tale" could be both "a true story" and "the unpainted seat of one's pants."

Two other research projects by Skinner into the sacred processes of poets are worth consulting: "The Alliteration in Shakespeare's Sonnets: A Study in Literary Behavior" and "A Quantitative Estimate of Certain Types of Sound-Patterning in Poetry," both of which are reprinted in the 1961 and

1972 editions of *Cumulative Record*. Surprisingly, Skinner demonstrated that there was no more alliteration in Shakespeare's sonnets than might be expected by chance. Then he went on, in a follow-up study, to show that Swinburne's poetry possessed a much higher "coefficient of alliteration" than Shakespeare's. Phrases such as "coefficient of alliteration" annoy those who believe that poetry is the voice of inspiration and is to be explicated only by ordained "critics." Behavioral approaches to the mysteries of poetry are not popular, and anyone who adopts such an approach can be expected to be accused of not knowing the difference between poets and pigeons, or between novelists and chimps.

12. *Walden Two* was rejected by two publishers before Macmillan published it in 1948. It took more than ten years for it to become a steady best-seller, but those who know the secrets of the book trade estimate that since then it has sold about 100,000 copies a year.

13. "The Phantom Plateau," *Journal of the Experimental Analysis of Behavior* 1 (1958), 1 - 13.

14. "B. F. Skinner . . . An Autobiography," in *Festschrift*, p. 16.

15. Ibid., See: *The Analysis of Behavior: A Programmed Text* (New York, 1961) and *The Technology of Teaching* (New York, 1968). The latter was appropriately dedicated to the memory of Skinner's beloved teacher, Mary I. Graves.

16. The wording of this citation is an interesting example of group verbal behavior. The word "despite," for example, introduces a statement that both apologizes for and explicates Skinner's "antitheoretical position." The passive "is considered" begs the question of who is doing the considering as well as weakening the praise. Also, note how 1958 Skinnerians were condemned with faint praise for predicting and controlling "the behavior of organisms from rat to man."

Chapter Two

1. Glenn Negley and J. Max Patrick, eds., *The Quest for Utopia: An Anthology of Imaginary Studies* (New York, 1952), p. 590. *Walden Two* has been attacked so often that predictably it is read as a dystopia by ingenuous readers, who then, of course, cannot attack it without endorsing Skinner. Sophisticated critics reject automation, engineering, and other attempts to cut down on tedious labor, frustration, and anxiety—in the name of humaneness. Such critics apparently glorify anguish as man's birthright. There is no point in multiplying examples of this kind of attack. Often, such charges against *Walden Two* are well meant, but they are functions of certain clearly definable convictions which have stood the test of the kind of time and the kind of controls not found in laboratories. The anxiety they reveal about any possible reduction in anxiety is symptomatic of humanism. Ostensibly on the side of courage, paradoxically they lack the courage to consider the possibility of cutting down on the need for so much courage.

2. *Walden Two* (New York, 1948, 1960, 1976). All references here are to the popular and widely distributed 1960 Macmillan paperback. Page references to quotations of any significant length are cited in parentheses after each quotation. The 1976 "reissue," in both hardcover and paper, contains a supportive commentary by Skinner and will eventually replace the earlier editions. References here to the 1960 paperback, however, are justified insofar as there may be well over a million copies of that edition already in the hands of potential users of this study.

3. Kathleen Kinkade, *A Walden Two Experiment: The First Five Years of Twin Oaks Community* (William Morrow, 1973), p. x. See also Skinner's commentary in the 1976 edition of *Walden Two*. In recent years Skinner has been less and less reluctant to talk about the significance of his novel. Obviously its popularity (both pros and cons have been *buying* it) has reinforced the author. He has lately unequivocally endorsed his early vision in general if not in particulars, advocating the development of small communities as alternatives to bankrupt and crowded cities. Skinner has resisted more and more the bigness of contemporary institutions without regressing to Thoreau's simplicity and pastoralism.

Chapter Three

1. *Science and Human Behavior* (New York, 1953), p. 449. (Subsequent page references to this work are cited in parentheses.) Skinner had few doubts of his own innocence when he wrote this book in 1953. Like John Watson he wanted "to know why men behave as they do." Also, of course, he realized that such knowledge would facilitate the controlling of behavior. In a real sense this work was the *first* attempt to reckon with the full significance of a functional analysis of human behavior. It was necessary, however, that essences and values be defined in terms of functions. Immediately, Skinner was accused of demeaning those essences and values. For example, to a scientist a man's "belief in God" may be an important and real factor in that man's life. The scientist neither denies nor affirms the existence of deities. The behavioral psychologist also finds "belief" relevant insofar as its consequences can be observed. Logically, this restriction should have pleased humanists, but they were uncomfortable because Skinner perceived religious institutions as reinforced and reinforcing *events*. Presumably he made no observations on the behavior of God for what to him seemed a quite obvious reason: There was no divine behavior to be observed.

2. See also, for further delightful observations on the training-of-animals routine, Skinner's essays: "How to Teach Animals" and "Pigeons in a Pelican" and "Squirrel in the Yard." The first two are reprinted in *Cumulative Record* (1961 and 1972) and the third in the 1972 edition only. Skinner has always been aware of certain ethical problems in training animals to perform complex acts, such as conditioning pigeons to pilot

bombs. He has recognized the "ethical question of our right to convert a lower creature into an unwitting hero. . . ."

3. Human subjects in the laboratory often cooperate with experimenters—especially with desperate graduate students collecting data for much-needed degrees—and begin to *report* seeing things that are not there. I once trained humans to *say* they saw lights at the end of a tube when there was no energy source to produce light. If I appeared anxious the subjects began to hallucinate lights. See: John A. Weigel, "Confession of a Verbal Behaviorist," *College Composition and Communication* 19 (October, 1968), 187 - 91.

Chapter Four

1. *The Behavior of Organisms* (New York, 1938), p. 442. Those "complexities" were comprehensively analyzed about twenty years later in *Verbal Behavior* (New York, 1957). I have relied on this 1957 work for my simplified outline of *how* "verbal behavior" differs from "language," the reading, writing, and talking of cognitive man. I have omitted many subtleties in order to focus on the controversial aspects of Skinner's treatment. (Subsequent page references to the 1957 text are cited in parentheses.)

2. This distinction is not easy to understand. The "unit" is an operant and as such it is defined in the context of *how* the response and the reinforcement relate to the stimulus.

3. See note 11, chapter 1 above.

4. Idem. To a behavioral scientist "inspirational" and "imaginative" may describe the end product, such as a fine poem, but they never describe the *cause* of that poem.

5. Noam Chomsky, "Review of B. F. Skinner's *Verbal Behavior*," *Language* 35 (1959), 26 - 58. This review has been reprinted several times and in 1967 Chomsky indicated he was still essentially satisfied with it.

6. Kenneth MacCorquodale, "On Chomsky's Review of Skinner's Verbal Behavior," *Journal of the Experimental Analysis of Behavior* 13 (1970), 83 - 99.

7. See, for example, Chomsky's review of Skinner's *Beyond Freedom and Dignity* in *The New York Review of Books*, December 30, 1971, p. 18.

8. MacCorquodale, p. 98. See also MacCorquodale's essay, "B. F. Skinner's *Verbal Behavior:* A Retrospective Appreciation," in *Festschrift for B. F. Skinner* (1970), pp. 340 - 50. In the 1970 essay MacCorquodale concedes only one "comfort" for those who "recoil from the conclusions in *Verbal Behavior*," namely, "the fact that Skinner cannot prove, any more than any other scientist can, that all the variance has been accounted for." Yet that residuum of variance need neither always go unaccounted for nor finally be credited to an autonomous factor. It is simply the as-yet-uncharted.

9. *The Technology of Teaching* (New York, 1968), p. 59. William James

is quoted by Skinner good-naturedly but Skinner firmly rejects the James-
ian compromise between science and the humanities, a compromise which
is still typical of many sincere intellectuals who continue to have conferences on the "relationship" between the two. Such symposiums usually
define areas of disagreement only and end in a superficially civilized agreement to continue to disagree.

    10. Ibid., p. 5.
    11. Ibid., p. 259.
    12. "What Is Psychotic Behavior?" in *Cumulative Record: A Selection of
Papers* (New York, 1972), p. 257.
    13. Ibid., p. 274.

Chapter Five

    1. *Beyond Freedom and Dignity* (New York, 1971), p. 215.
    2. Mary Harrington Hall, "An Interview with 'Mr. Behaviorist,' "
Psychology Today 1 (September, 1967), 21 - 23, 68 - 7.
    3. Richard I. Evans, *B. F. Skinner: The Man and His Ideas* (New York,
1968), pp. 103, 107, 120 - 21.
    4. *Contingencies of Reinforcement: A Theoretical Analysis* (New York,
1969). By 1969 Skinner was ready to modify his antitheory position. His
1950 essay "Are Theories of Learning Necessary?" had stereotyped him as
a "Grand Anti-Theoretician." He admits this new work is "theoretical in
several senses. . . ." Yet he has continued to minimize the significance of
"hypothetico-deductive methods."
    5. Ibid., p. 296. That fact, more precisely, *is* phylogenic contingency. To
debate whether the species has survived or has not is silly. *One is* and *we
are*, and something happened to make "it" so. That something is contingency to Skinner. Of course, God could be contingent upon our need for
Him just as Skinner was contingent upon my need for him. Professor
Skinner, however, says I did not invent him. I happened to be there
(Columbia University) one summer (1947) when he was. *I* pressed the
lever: *he* was my reward. (Subsequent page references to *Contingencies of
Reinforcement* are cited in parentheses.)
    6. Skinner's *Beyond Freedom and Dignity* (New York, 1971) was not un-
predictable to anyone who over the years had been following his work and
noting the implications. The book was a bomb (a harmless stink bomb to
many, but a nuclear threat to others) only to newcomers to the Skinnerian
scene. Because this study is limited in space and because I have tried to
prepare the occasion for this work, I have focused on its challenging aspects
and neglected much of the understructure—some of which is understandably redundant. (Subsequent page references to this work are cited in
parentheses.)
    7. The fear of control and all that it implies was part of the sincere rejec-
tion of *Beyond Freedom and Dignity*, but politicians and other propagan-

dizers who defend "liberty" as a shibboleth had a field day denouncing Skinner. Because the hostile reviewers and critics—even the sincere ones—cannot refute Skinner *scientifically* without stooping to what they are denouncing, eloquent rhetoric takes over, with much repetition of the axiom that man cannot be measured, that freedom and dignity are intuitively real, that the human conscience is a responsible autonomous agent, etc. Skinner's sometime answers to his critics eventually emerge as his next book, which is discussed here. See, however, for his 1973 "position" the brief but cogent essay, "Answers for My Critics," in Harvey Wheeler, ed., *Beyond the Primitive Society* (San Francisco, 1973).

8. *About Behaviorism* (New York, 1974), p. 3. A paperback edition is also now available (Vintage Books) with several cover blurbs that are certainly meant to placate potential readers who might have found *Beyond Freedom and Dignity* offensive. For example, one extract from a review by Robert Kirsch in the *Los Angeles Times* states that this book is "much more effective" than its predecessor "precisely because it takes more seriously the tradition (or the historical prejudices) of its opposition." (Subsequent page references to *About Behaviorism* are cited in parentheses.)

9. "Skinner's Utopia: Panacea or Path to Hell?" *Time* (September 20, 1971), pp. 354 - 71. See also *Time* (January 17, 1972), p. 2, for the report on the poll of Skinner's popularity.

Selected Bibliography

PRIMARY SOURCES

Many important articles, reports, and essays by Skinner eventually were expanded or combined into book-length works as the ideas became refined and more fully documented. There is no need to complicate this bibliography by listing these shorter pieces separately and redundantly. Other important shorter writings have been included by Skinner in the two available editions of his *Cumulative Record* listed below. The numerous items in these collections have also not been listed separately except in the *Notes and References* above whenever they were referred to in the text. For a complete bibliography of Skinner's writings up to *Contingencies of Reinforcement* (1969) see *Festschrift for B. F. Skinner*, ed. P. D. Dews (New York: Appleton-Century-Crofts, 1970). This volume also contains a reprint of Skinner's short autobiography which is being superseded by a much longer version presently in progress. In order to facilitate the general reader's investigation of Skinner's basic writings it seemed best to include here, for the above reasons, only the book-length works now available. (Many of these are also available in paperback but are not listed here because public and academic libraries usually contain only the hardcover editions.)

The Behavior of Organisms. New York: Appleton-Century-Crofts, 1938.
Walden Two. New York: The Macmillan Company, 1948.
Science and Human Behavior. New York: The Macmillan Company, 1953.
Schedules of Reinforcement (with C. B. Ferster). New York: Appleton-Century-Crofts, 1957.
Verbal Behavior. New York: Appleton-Century-Crofts, 1957.
The Analysis of Behavior (a programmed text with J. G. Holland). New York: McGraw Hill, 1961.
Cumulative Record. New York: Appleton-Century-Crofts, 1961.
The Technology of Teaching. New York: Appleton-Century-Crofts, 1968.

Contingencies of Reinforcement: A Theoretical Analysis. New York: Appleton-Century-Crofts, 1969.

Beyond Freedom and Dignity. New York: Alfred A. Knopf, 1971.

Cumulative Record: A Selection of Papers. New York: Appleton-Century-Crofts, 1972.

About Behaviorism. New York: Alfred A. Knopf, 1974.

Particulars of My Life. New York: Alfred A. Knopf, 1976.

SECONDARY SOURCES

1. Reviews, Interviews, Tributes, and Critiques

ANON. "Doing without Conscience." *The Times Literary Supplement,* May 12, 1972, pp. 533 - 34. The apparently British author of this review of *Beyond Freedom and Dignity* concludes that Skinner is a typical American, that is, an optimistic technocrat. He credits him, nevertheless, with "intelligence and sophisticated acumen."

CARPENTER, FINLEY. *The Skinner Primer: Beyond Freedom and Dignity.* New York: The Free Press, 1974. The publisher's attempt to promote this book as "an interesting companion piece" to Skinner's work is more venal than Carpenter's good intentions deserve. Yet the conclusion of this criticism of Skinner's position is untenable. Carpenter would accept Skinner if the latter would accept "cognitive freedom," which to a pure behaviorist would be as incomprehensible as a mere touch of pregnancy to a pure woman.

CHOMSKY, NOAM. "Review of B. F. Skinner's *Verbal Behavior.*" *Language* 35 (1959), 26 - 58. This famous essay allegedly demolished Skinner, although Skinner needed to read only part of it before deciding that Chomsky did not understand him. It has been reprinted several times and "answered" by Kenneth MacCorquodale (see below), but the issues are still abrasive on both sides.

_____. "The Case Against B. F. Skinner." *The New York Review of Books,* December 30, 1971, p. 18. The title of this essay promises something more than a review of Skinner's *Beyond Freedom and Dignity,* and in fact it is an acidulous second major attack on Skinner's ideas and an attempt to score points with clever phrases such as accusing Skinner of not knowing the difference between pigeons and poets. This charge is perhaps a refinement on Chomsky's earlier assumption that Skinner did not know the difference between ordinary people and rats. Chomskyites hugely admire this essay, which this time Skinner himself more or less answered in *About Behaviorism.*

DEWS, P. B., ed. *Festschrift for B. F. Skinner.* New York: Appleton-Century-Crofts, 1970. These thirty-six essays, according to the editor, which "are dedicated to one of the great men of our times on his sixty-fifth birthday . . . are a highly selected more or less random collection of contributions to fields started by B. F. Skinner." The volume also includes a reprint of Skinner's autobiographical sketch and an essay by Kenneth MacCorquodale in appreciation of Skinner's *Verbal Behavior* as well as samples of the increasingly sophisticated work of students and colleagues.

DOWLING, WILLIAM F. "Conversations with B. F. Skinner." *Organizational Dynamics* 1 (Winter, 1973), 31 - 40. The interviewer probes Skinner for possible applications of the scientist's ideas to business and finds them useful and potentially profitable, although Skinner seems to have remained ethically neutral about the interviewer's venality. Skinner says, among other things, that he has never confused industrial workers with his pigeons.

EVANS, RICHARD I. *B. F. Skinner, the Man and His Ideas.* New York: E. P. Dutton, 1968. Edited tapes of interviews with Skinner are adapted to a series which, according to Evans, was meant to feature primarily "personality psychologists." Evans, with some condescension, finds Skinner's psychology "the most significant alternative to a personality psychology." Although Skinner's own words are probably reliably reported, the conclusion that Professor Skinner is really a good humanist is not warranted by the evidence here presented; yet withal it is a friendly book—and thus rare.

FRIEDRICHS, ROBERT W. "The Potential Impact of B. F. Skinner Upon American Sociology." *The American Sociologist* 9 (February, 1974), 3 - 8. Friedrichs warns that Skinner's "imagery . . . reflects the paternalistic transposition of a Calvinist communitarianism into a cybernetic secularism, with program-bearing behavioral scientists standing as 'functional equivalents' to scripture-bearing men of the cloth." Which is probably translatable as: "Watch out for this man Skinner!"

FULLER, PAUL R. "Professors Kantor and Skinner—the 'Grand Alliance' of the 40's." *The Psychological Record* 23 (1973), 318 - 24. The result of the interaction between Kantor and Skinner at Indiana University beginning in 1945 was stimulating to both men and enriching to their students. Although Skinnerians were generally younger and less philosophical than Kantorians, they were all more or less realists and strengthened one another's weaknesses.

HALL, MARY HARRINGTON. "An Interview with 'Mr. Behaviorist' B. F. Skinner." *Psychology Today* 1 (September, 1967), 21 - 33, 68 - 71. "If I could do it all over again," Skinner confides to his charming and not unfriendly but strictly slick-professional interviewer, "I'd never teach those pigeons to play Ping Pong." As usual, Mr. Behaviorist politely, patiently, and efficiently explicates and defends his position. This is one of the "interviews" which predict Skinner's *willingness* (if such a word may be used in reference to an honest behaviorist) to participate in talk shows and otherwise help promote his ideas—and sell his books. Withal, however, Skinner manages to "lose" most TV debates to emotionalists while winning increasing respect from his converts, which is a rather subtle kind of success insuring him the continued love of those who distrust talk shows and commercial promotions.

KINKADE, KATHLEEN. *A Walden Two Experiment* (with foreword by B. F. Skinner). New York: William Morrow, 1973. The first five years of a serious effort to set up a Walden Two (Twin Oaks, Virginia) is evaluated by a founding member, who concludes that the experiment had not yet resulted in "a real Walden Two." For example, children were excluded. Yet Skinner's brief foreword is supportive and optimistic, predicting his increasing concern for applications of his ideas in "real" life.

KRUTCH, JOSEPH WOOD. *The Measure of Man.* New York: Bobbs-Merrill, 1954. This all-out attack, followed by years of repeating the same complaints against Skinner in numerous places, typifies the sincere humanistic abhorrence of behavioral engineering, which was understandably reinforced during World War II by fascist and communist abuses of psychological know-how. All in all, however, Krutch and other well meaning critics react to the possible *abuses* of knowledge rather than to knowledge itself and in their anxious fear of anyone "measuring man" ethically or psychologically they would allow no man to measure any man for any purpose. Their prototype is Job, who accepted the mystery of life as beyond his ken. Perhaps they also secretly expect that their goods will be restored to them, as Job's goods were restored to him, for remaining ignorant. Krutch has been one of Skinner's most distinguished and persistently hostile critics. The respect he has earned in other arenas has carried over and underwritten his less enlightened attacks on Skinner.

LEHMANN-HAUPT, CHRISTOPHER. "It's a Wonderful Life." *The New York Times*, March 26, 1976, p. 33. Although this reviewer of Skinner's autobiographical *Particulars of My Life* is "charmed by the warm boy-growing-up-in-small-town-American simplicity" of the book, he identifies "a negative side to the discovery of Skinner's humanity." He sees evidence for the origin of Skinner's "radically empirical scientist" in his youthful "obsession with gadgetry." Need more be said about how the questions are begged when Skinner is the subject? (What *caused* Skinner's obsession with gadgetry other than his potential genius for becoming an empirical scientist?)

MACCORQUODALE, KENNETH. "On Chomsky's Review of Skinner's *Verbal Behavior*." *Journal of the Experimental Analysis of Behavior* 13 (1970), 83 - 99. This careful and relatively dispassionate answer to Chomsky's review some years before, clearly defines the issue as the old environment-versus-heredity debate, with Chomsky claiming the

genetic structures in verbalizing as the prime cause and Skinner putting the emphasis on the environment. Chomsky "wins" intuitively
only because intuition is not part of the behaviorist's repertoire, and
MacCorquodale neither wins nor loses, for only experimentation
counts, and verbal behavior is still largely unexplored except
speculatively. Withal, MacCorquodale has done a much-needed ser-
vice to Skinner, for prior to this essay even ardent behaviorists were
troubled by the arguments of structuralists against Skinner's *Verbal
Behavior*. It does seem that every possible combination of verbal
units could not be separately reinforced. Now behaviorists understand
that there need not be deep, mysterious structures at work in the
human psyche to account for languages.

MACHAN, THOR R. *The Pseudo-Science of B. F. Skinner*. New Rochelle:
Arlington House Publishers, 1974. Typical of the hostility toward
Skinner expressed by those who defend the right to liberty and
private property "in the name of God," this essay ardently opposes
Skinner's reductive materialism and—quite reductively itself—
denounces Skinner as dangerous.

SENNET, RICHARD. "Beyond Freedom and Dignity." *The New York Times
Book Review*, October 24, 1971, pp. 1, 12 - 16. The reviewer accuses
Skinner of confirming the stereotype of social scientists as "dogmatic
and naive" and of personally being "a very troubled behaviorist"
who "doesn't believe in his own utopia," thus revealing the critic's
ignorance of behaviorism, in which doing is the only test of believing. Such critiques cast Skinner in the role of prophet precisely to the
extent that they suppose he must be suffering.

TODD, RICHARD. " 'Walden Two': Three? Many More?" *The New York
Times Magazine*, March 15, 1970, pp. 24 - 25, 114 - 23. In this il-
lustrated and early account of the Twin Oaks experiment Todd clearly indicates Skinner's growing involvement in "alternative life styles"
as well as his bemused acceptance of the repeated attacks of critics
such as Joseph Wood Krutch (see above).

WANN, T. W., ed. *Behaviorism and Phenomenology: Contrasting Bases for
Modern Psychology*. Chicago: The University of Chicago Press,
1964. This significant collection of papers from a symposium contains
Skinner's essay "Behaviorism at Fifty," in which the author rather
coolly admits "mental processes" as possible data for behaviorism
when "formulated in effective ways." Later he made quite clear that
what he meant by "effective ways" still ruled out fictions such as
"will."

WHEELER, HARVEY, ed. *Beyond the Punitive Society*. San Francisco: W. H.
Freeman, 1973. This collection of mostly nonhostile essays responds
to the implications of Skinner's *Beyond Freedom and Dignity*.
Appended is an essay by Skinner himself, "Answers for My Critics,"
which predicts his 1974 book-length explication, *About Behaviorism*.

Some Skinnerians may have been saddened when their master stooped to answering his carping critics, yet in all good faith the time had come to try to inform if not placate the hostile. Although behaviorists do *know* that persuasion is ineffective without reinforcement they also know that to respond to one's critics is not only polite but also inevitable.

2. General References

CHEIN, ISADOR. *The Science of Behavior and the Image of Man*. New York: Basic Books, 1972. Although Chein sees man as an "active, responsible agent" he still identifies with determinism and materialism: an example of trying to defeat your Skinner and still have him too.

HULL, CLARK L. *Principles of Behavior*. New York: Appleton-Century, 1943. Like Skinner's *The Behavior of Organisms* (1938) and Tolman's *Purposive Behavior in Animals and Man* (1932), Hull's work underwrote a version of American behaviorism. Hull was, however, the most theoretical and thus in some ways the most formidable of the three scientists. Allegiances to Hull have been almost as loyal as those to Skinner, although Hull did not generate as much hostility.

KAREN, ROBERT L. *An Introduction to Behavior Theory and Its Applications*. New York: Harper and Row, 1974. The "primary source of information" in this text, according to the author, "is the writings of B. F. Skinner and his students." An example of how Skinner's "guarded guesses" have been adopted by others, this book, although understandably slanted to undergraduates, represents one of the ways Skinner has entered the average classroom via those not hostile to behaviorism. Although "behavioral science" departments now may outnumber "psychology departments" in American colleges, all is not Skinnerian that calls itself behavioral.

KLEIN, D. B. *A History of Scientific Psychology*. New York and London: Basic Books, 1970. This survey of the history of the efforts of psychology to achieve "scientific status" identifies Skinner as "a radical behaviorist" whose "operationism is to be viewed as belonging to the Watsonian tradition." For those who do not understand events until they are put in historical contexts this account may be helpful. It does, however, also put Skinner in a context and thus, intentionally or not, diminishes his heroism.

KOESTLER, ARTHUR. *The Ghost in the Machine*. New York: The Macmillan Company, 1968. Koestler asserts that "science has forgotten to ask the pertinent questions—or refused to ask them on the pretext that they are meaningless." He has proudly been one of the main opponents of behaviorism but unfortunately, like too many others he stoops to name-calling. As expected, he charges that Skinner prefers rats to men. This is the kind of simplification that invalidates the critic's good intentions. Ironically, Skinner-baiting only provides Skinner with further evidence that even good men are conditioned rather than rational.

LEIBER, JUSTIN. *Noam Chomsky: A Philosophic Overview.* Boston: Twayne Publishers, 1975. This philosopher's judicious and dispassionate explication of Chomsky's ideas is an indispensable reference book for anyone concerned about the Chomsky-Skinner debate at the dignified level of empiricism versus rationalism. Chomsky would do well to rest his case with Leiber, who is possibly a better apologist for Chomsky's cause than he is himself.

MATSON, FLOYD. *The Broken Image: Man, Science, and Society.* New York: Braziller, 1964. Objecting to Skinner's "deep urge not only to observe men behaving but to *make* them behave," Matson denounces *Walden Two* as a description of a dystopia. He stands with James Wood Krutch (see above) and Arthur Koestler (see above) as archenemies of Skinner's behaviorism. (That men should be kept from observing men so that men may not control men implies endorsement of medievalism. Galileo, frightened for his life, once denied the evidence of his senses as magnified by his telescope, but that was a long time ago and in a different country.)

NEGLEY, GLENN, and J. MAX PATRICK, eds. *The Quest for Utopia: An Anthology of Imaginary Societies.* New York: Henry Schuman, 1952. A professor of philosophy and a professor of English find Skinner's *Walden Two* nauseating and blasphemous, concluding that it represents "a nadir of ignominy." Needless to add, they are both antibehaviorists.

RACHLIN, HOWARD. *Introduction to Modern Behaviorism.* San Francisco: W. H. Freeman, 1970. "The main purpose of this volume," the author says, "is simply to give the reader an idea of what sort of things psychologists who call themselves behaviorists do and why they do them." Inevitably the *what* is more easily described than the *why*. Anyway, too much space and time have been wasted in inventing fictions to answer *why* questions. It happens, Skinner says, or it does not. Only the coordinates of the happening can be said to account for it. Behaviorism emerged after other ways had become less and less effective to certain scientists who again are testing "it" for effectiveness—depending upon one's definition of effective. (Insanity can be very effective if one "needs" to be insane; so can dying if one "needs" to be dead.)

SPENCE, K. W. *Behavior Theory and Conditioning.* New Haven: Yale University Press, 1956. Spence, who died in 1967, is associated with "neobehaviorism," which acknowledges personal observation as the basic datum, preferably expressed in physicalist terms. Unlike Skinner's behaviorism, the neomethodology relies on deduction more often than radical positivists would allow. Neobehaviorism, however, despite the unfortunate connotation of the term, shares non-neobehaviorism's faith in "reality." (Mayhap the late 1970s will be the end of the "dark ages" and informed humans will stop debating about how many—and why—behaviorists can fit into a Skinner box.)

TOLMAN, EDWARD CHACE. *Behavior and Psychological Man.* Los Angeles: University of California Press, 1951. This is another rat psychologist's "ratiocinations," but with a difference: more purposiveness and more cognition. Tolman's "work" has been overshadowed by Skinner's for a good reason. Although Skinner has been less genial he has been more scientific. The Skinnerian austerity has lost him friends but gained him facts.

WATSON, JOHN B. *Behaviorism.* Chicago: The University of Chicago Press, 1924 (new edition, 1958). Cited as "the book that initiated a revolution to make psychology an objective science," Watson's manifesto is still the purest—and thus the most untenable—example of behaviorism. "Let us," he said quite simply, "limit ourselves to things that can be observed and formulate laws only according to those things." Skinner's "operant conditioning" now accounts for all Watson had hoped to account for but really could not as long as he simplified conditioning.

WEIGEL, JOHN A. "Confession of a Verbal Behaviorist." *College Composition and Communication* 19 (October, 1968), 187 - 91. The author of this study summarizes the implications of a friendly conversion to Skinnerian behaviorism in 1947 (unknown at that time to Professor Skinner) followed by the discovery that the safest way to distinguish between rats and humans in the Columbia University laboratories was *not* to ask them what they were, for humans are conditioned to lie and rats either cannot talk or do not choose to do so. This is a heartfelt confession of what can happen to an ingenuous professor of literature when he first encounters those who believe in facts rather than in fictions.

ZOELLNER, ROBERT. "Talk-Write: A Behavioral Pedagogy for Composition." *College English* 30 (January, 1969), 267 - 320. Applying the principles of Skinner's operant learning, Zoellner projects an ideal program for teaching college composition. He defends behaviorism but describes his own "extrapolations" therefrom as "rodential" rather than Skinnerian, rejecting Skinner's "tact-mand schema" as untenable. Thus in effect he denies his Skinner while building upon him. (How many disciples must deny a prophet while exploiting his teachings before the betrayers join together and become a venerated social institution?)

Index

(The works of B. F. Skinner are listed under his name.)